GRADES K-2

...the Super Source®
Color Tiles

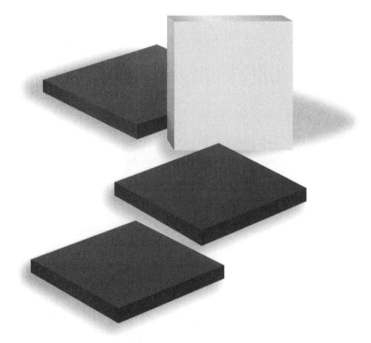

ETA/Cuisenaire®
Vernon Hills, Illinois 60061-1862

800-445-5985

www.etacuisenaire.com

Cuisenaire extends its warmest thanks to the many teachers and students across the country who helped ensure the success of the Super Source® series by participating in the outlining, writing, and field testing of the materials.

Project Director: Judith Adams
Managing Editor: Doris Hirschhorn
Editorial Team: Patricia Kijak Anderson, Linda Dodge, John Nelson, Deborah J. Slade, Harriet Slonim
Field Test Coordinator: Laurie Verdeschi

Design Manager: Phyllis Aycock
Text Design: Amy Berger, Tracey Munz
Line Art and Production: Joan Lee, Fiona Santoianni
Cover Design: Michael Muldoon
Illustrations: Rebecca Thornburgh

...the Super Source®

Table of Contents

Using the Super Source

The Super Source™ is a series of books each of which contains a collection of activities to use with a specific math manipulative. Driving **the Super Source™** is Cuisenaire's conviction that children construct their own understandings through rich, hands-on mathematical experiences. Although the activities in each book are written for a specific grade range, they all connect to the core of mathematics learning that is important to every K-6 child. Thus, the material in many activities can easily be refocused for children at other grade levels. Because the activities are not arranged sequentially, children can work on any activity at any time.

The lessons in **the Super Source™** all follow a basic structure consistent with the vision of mathematics teaching described in the *Curriculum and Evaluation Standards for School Mathematics* published by the National Council of Teachers of Mathematics.

All of the activities in this series involve Problem Solving, Communication, Reasoning, and Mathematical Connections—the first four NCTM Standards. Each activity also focuses on one or more of the following curriculum strands: Number, Geometry, Measurement, Patterns/Functions, Probability/Statistics, Logic.

HOW LESSONS ARE ORGANIZED

At the beginning of each lesson, you will find, to the right of the title, both the major curriculum strands to which the lesson relates and the particular topics that children will work with. Each lesson has three main sections. The first, GETTING READY, offers an *Overview*, which states what children will be doing, and why, and a list of "What You'll Need." Specific numbers of Color Tiles are suggested on this list but can be adjusted as the needs of your specific situation dictate. Before an activity, tiles can be counted out and placed in containers or self-sealing plastic bags for easy distribution. When crayons are called for, it is understood that their colors are those that match the Color Tiles and that markers may be used in place of crayons. Blackline masters that are provided for your convenience at the back of the book are referenced on this list. Paper, pencils, scissors, tape, and materials for making charts, which are necessary in certain activities, are usually not.

Although overhead Color Tiles and the suggestion to make overhead transparencies of the blackline masters are always listed in "What You'll Need" as optional, these materials are highly effective when you want to demonstrate the use of Color Tiles. As you move the tiles on the screen, children can work with the same materials at their seats. Children can also use the overhead to present their work to other members of their group or to the class.

The second section, THE ACTIVITY, first presents a possible scenario for *Introducing* the children to the activity. The aim of this brief introduction is to help you give children the tools they will need to investigate independently. However, care has been taken to avoid undercutting the activity itself. Since these investigations are designed to enable children to increase their own mathematical power, the idea is to set the stage but not steal the show! The heart of the lesson, *On Their Own*, is found in a box at the top of the second page of each lesson. Here, rich problems stimulate many different problem-solving approaches and lead to a variety of solutions. These hands-on explorations have the potential for bringing children to new mathematical ideas and deepening skills.

On Their Own is intended as a stand-alone activity for children to explore with a partner or in a small group. Be sure to make the needed directions clearly visible. You may want to write them on the chalkboard or on an overhead or present them either on reusable cards or paper. For children who may have difficulty reading the directions, you can read them aloud or make sure that at least one "reader" is in each group.

The last part of this second section, *The Bigger Picture*, gives suggestions for how children can share their work and their thinking and make mathematical connections. Class charts and children's recorded work provide a springboard for discussion. Under "Thinking and Sharing," there are several prompts that you can use to promote discussion. Children will not be able to respond to these prompts with one-word answers. Instead, the prompts encourage children to describe what they notice, tell how they found their results and give the reasoning behind their answers. Thus children learn to verify their own results rather than relying on the teacher to determine if an answer is "right" or "wrong." Though the class discussion might immediately follow the investigation, it is important not to cut the activity short by having a class discussion too soon.

The Bigger Picture often includes a suggestion for a "Writing" (or drawing) assignment. This is meant to help children process what they have just been doing. You might want to use these ideas as a focus for daily or weekly entries in a math journal that each child keeps.

The hardest thing about being the designer was uslaning the derzion. I like the game because it was fun and not to easy like some things are.

From: *Follow Me*

Make all of your 7's go on the side of the paper not in the middel because then all of the places don't get filled.

From: *Square by Square*

The Bigger Picture always ends with ideas for "Extending the Activity." Extensions take the essence of the main activity and either alter or extend its parameters. These activities are well used with a class that becomes deeply involved in the primary activity or for children who finish before the others. In any case, it is probably a good idea to expose the entire class to the possibility of, and the results from, such extensions.

The third and final section of the lesson is TEACHER TALK. Here, in *Where's the Mathematics?*, you can gain insight into the underlying mathematics of the activity and discover some of the strategies children are apt to use as they work. Solutions are also given—when such are necessary and/or helpful. Because *Where's the Mathematics?* provides a view of what may happen in the lesson as well as the underlying mathematical potential that may grow out of it, this may be the section that you want to read before presenting the activity to children.

USING THE ACTIVITIES

The Super Source™ has been designed to fit into the variety of classroom environments in which it will be used. These range from a completely manipulative-based classroom to one in which manipulatives are just beginning to play a part. You may choose to use some activities in *the Super Source*™ in the way set forth in each lesson (introducing an activity to the whole class, then breaking the class up into groups that all work on the same task, and so forth). You will then be able to circulate among the groups as they work to observe and perhaps comment on each child's work. This approach requires a full classroom set of materials but allows you to concentrate on the variety of ways that children respond to a given activity.

Alternatively, you may wish to make two or three related activities available to different groups of children at the same time. You may even wish to use different manipulatives to explore the same mathematical concept. (Cuisenaire® Rods and Snap™ Cubes, for example, can be used to teach some of the same concepts as Color Tiles.) This approach does not require full classroom sets of a particular manipulative. It also permits greater adaptation of materials to individual children's needs and/or preferences.

If children are comfortable working independently, you might want to set up a "menu"— that is, set out a number of related activities from which children can choose. Children should be encouraged to write about their experiences with these independent activities.

However you choose to use *the Super Source*™ activities, it would be wise to allow time for several groups or the entire class to share their experiences. The dynamics of this type of interaction, in which children share not only solutions and strategies but also feelings and intuitions, is the basis of continued mathematical growth. It allows children who are beginning to form a mathematical structure to clarify it and those who have mastered just isolated concepts to begin to see how these concepts might fit together.

Again, both the individual teaching style and combined learning styles of the children should dictate the specific method of utilizing *the Super Source*™ lessons. At first sight, some activities may appear too difficult for some of your children, and you may find yourself tempted to actually "teach" by modeling exactly how an activity can lead to a particular learning outcome. If you do this, you rob children of the chance to try the activity in whatever way they can. As long as children have a way to begin an investigation, give them time and opportunity to see it through. Instead of making assumptions about what children will or won't do, watch and listen. The excitement and challenge of the activity—as well as the chance to work cooperatively—may bring out abilities in children that will surprise you.

If you are convinced, however, that an activity does not suit your students, adjust it, by all means. You may want to change the language, either by simplifying it or by referring to specific vocabulary that you and your children already use and are comfortable with. On the other hand, if you suspect that an activity is not challenging enough, you may want to read through the activity extensions for a variation that you can give children instead.

RECORDING

Although the direct process of working with Color Tiles is a valuable one, it is afterward, when children look at, compare, share, and think about their work, that an activity yields its greatest rewards. However, because Color Tile designs can't always be left intact, children need an effective way to record their work. To this end, at the back of this book recording paper is provided for reproduction. The "What You'll Need" listing at the beginning of each lesson often specifies the kind of recording paper to use. For example, it seems natural for children to record Color Tile patterns on grid paper. Yet it is important for children to use a method of recording that they feel comfortable with. Frustration in recording their structures can leave children feeling that the actual activity was either too difficult or just not fun! Thus, there may be times when you feel children should just share their work rather than record it.

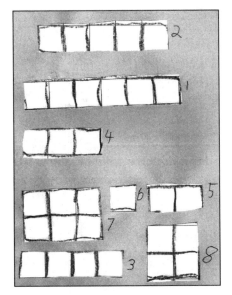

From: *How Many Rectangles?*

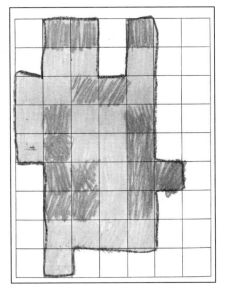

From: *Half and Half*

Young children might duplicate their work on grid paper by coloring in boxes on grids that exactly match the tiles in size. Older children may be able to use smaller grids or even construct the recording paper as they see fit.

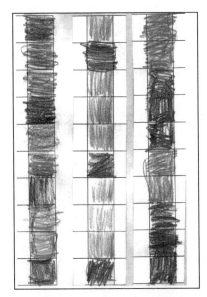

From: *Creating Patterns*

From: *Creature Feature*

Another interesting way to "freeze" a Color Tile design is to create it using a software piece, and then get a printout. Children can use a classroom or resource-room computer if it is available or, where possible, extend the activity into a home assignment by utilizing their home computers.

Recording involves more than copying designs. Writing, drawing, and making charts and tables are also ways to record. By creating a table of data gathered in the course of their investigations, children are able to draw conclusions and look for patterns. When children write or draw, either in their group or later by themselves, they are clarifying their understanding of their recent mathematical experience.

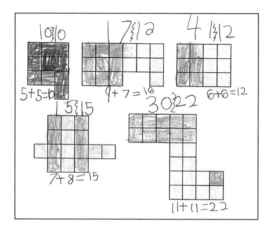

From: *Half and Half*

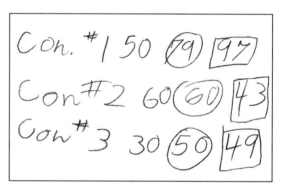

From: *Estimation Jars*

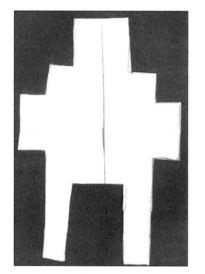

From: *Mirror, Mirror on the Wall*

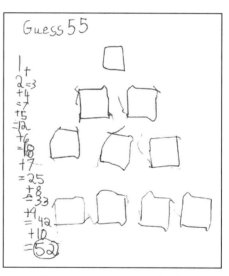

From: *Very Busy Animals*

With a roomful of children busily engaged in their investigations, it is not easy for a teacher to keep track of how individual children are working. Having tangible material to gather and examine when the time is right will help you to keep in close touch with each child's learning.

Exploring Color Tiles

Color Tiles are a versatile collection of 1-inch square tiles which come in four colors—red, green, yellow, and blue. They are pleasant to handle and easy to manipulate. Children can use the tiles to act out story problems involving all sorts of everyday objects. Learning to use small colored squares to represent such objects is a significant step in the process of learning to abstract.

Although Color Tiles are simple in concept, they can be used to develop a wide variety of mathematical ideas at many different levels of complexity. Young children who start using Color Tiles to make patterns may be likely to talk about numbers of different-colored tiles. Some children may even spontaneously begin to count and compare numbers. The fact that the tiles are squares means that they fit naturally into a grid pattern, and when Color Tiles are used on top of a printed grid—for example, a number chart—the tiles can be used to discover many number patterns. As they record their patterns, children are also using their spatial skills and strategies to locate positions of particular tiles.

> I would count the amount I was taking before I took the amount.

From: *Last Survivor*

When making patterns, children often provide the best inspiration for one another. Given sufficient time, some child will come up with an idea that excites the imagination of other children. It is preferable that new ideas arise in this way, because then children develop confidence in their own abilities to be creative. Though children need to explore patterns freely, some children may also appreciate challenges, such as being asked to make patterns with certain types of symmetry or patterns with certain characteristics, such as specific colors that represent different fractional parts.

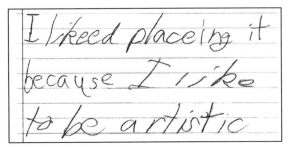

> I likeed placeing it becayse I like to be artistic

From: *Mirror, Mirror on the Wall*

Logical thinking is always involved when children investigate Color Tile patterns, because, in order to recognize and continue a visual pattern, children must form conjectures, verify them, and then apply them.

WORKING WITH COLOR TILES

As counters, Color Tiles are very important early number models. Eventually children will develop more abstract concepts of numbers and will not be dependent on manipulation of objects. Color Tiles can help children build such abstract structures.

The tiles fall naturally into certain patterns, as shown below, and enable children to visualize the relationships as represented by the tiles.

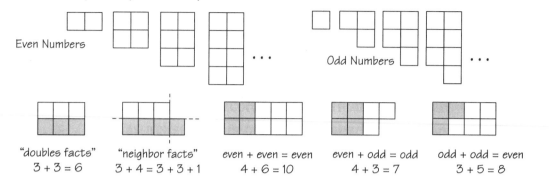

"doubles facts"	"neighbor facts"	even + even = even	even + odd = odd	odd + odd = even
3 + 3 = 6	3 + 4 = 3 + 3 + 1	4 + 6 = 10	4 + 3 = 7	3 + 5 = 8

Since there are large numbers of them, Color Tiles are useful for estimation and developing number sense. Children can take a handful, estimate how many, then separate the tiles into rows of ten to identify how many "tens" and how many "ones" there are. The colors of the tiles also make them useful in developing the concept of place value. For example, children can play exchange games in which each color tile represents a place value—ones, tens, hundreds, and thousands. Exchange games can work for subtraction as well as addition, and can also refer to decimals, where tile colors would represent units, tenths, hundredths, and thousandths.

Color Tiles are very suitable for developing an understanding of the meaning of addition. The sum 2 + 3 can be modeled by taking two tiles of one color and three of another, and then counting them. Subtraction problems can also be modeled either traditionally—put up five tiles and take two away—or by taking five tiles of one color, then covering two with a different color so that it is obvious that three tiles of the original color are left. Either of these methods of modeling makes the connection between addition and subtraction apparent.

Color Tiles are also ideal for developing the concept of multiplication, both as grouping and as an array. To show 3 x 4, children can make three groups with four tiles in each group and then arrange them in a rectangular array of three rows of four tiles. The advantage of the array is that by turning it children can see that 3 x 4 = 4 x 3. The array model also leads naturally into the development of the formula for the area of the rectangle. In fact, Color Tiles are especially suitable for exploring all area and perimeter relations.

Color Tiles can be used to explore all the different ways that squares can be arranged, subject to certain constraints. One classic investigation is to find all "tetraminoes," "pentominoes," and "hexominoes," that is, all ways to arrange either four, five, or six tiles respectively, so that one complete side of each tile touches at least one complete side of another tile. Color Tiles can be used to investigate how many different rectangular arrays a given number of tiles can have. This helps children to discover that for some numbers—prime numbers—the only possible rectangular arrays are one-tile wide. At an upper-grade level, the colors of tiles can represent prime numbers, and a set of tiles can be used to represent the prime factorization of a number. For example, if a red tile represents 2 and a green tile represents 3, the number 24 might be represented by three red tiles and one green tile, since 24 = 2 x 2 x 2 x 3. This representation of numbers in terms of factors can help children to understand procedures for finding greatest common divisors and least common multiples. Since the Color Tiles all feel exactly the same, they can be used to provide hands-on experience with sampling. By using a collection of tiles in a bag, children can investigate how repeated sampling, with replacement, can be used to predict the contents of the bag. Since the tiles are square, they can also be used to represent entries in a bar graph drawn on 1-inch grid paper. For example, class opinion polls can be quickly conducted by having each child place a tile in the column on a graph which corresponds to his or her choice.

To stimulate algebraic thinking, number sentences can be introduced in which each number is covered with tiles. The challenge for children is to figure out what is under each tile. Children will learn that sometimes they can be sure of the number covered, as in $4 + \boxed{} = 6$, while at other times they cannot, as in $\boxed{} + \boxed{} = 6$. This use of tiles lays the groundwork for introducing a variable.

ASSESSING CHILDREN'S UNDERSTANDING

Color Tiles are wonderful tools for assessing children's mathematical thinking. Watching children work with their Color Tiles gives you a sense of how they approach a mathematical problem. Their thinking can be "seen," in so far as that thinking is expressed through the way they construct, recognize, and continue spatial patterns. When a class breaks up into small working groups, you are able to circulate, listen, and raise questions, all the while focusing on how individuals are thinking. Here is a perfect opportunity for authentic assessment.

Having children describe their designs and share their strategies and thinking with the whole class gives you another opportunity for observational assessment. Furthermore, you may want to gather children's recorded work or invite them to choose pieces to add to their math portfolios.

> I thought Yellow came in first because. It was the biggest. Green was in second place. And red came in Third place. And blue came last.

From: *Counting Colors*

> yealy recktangles with 6 tiles are bigger then other recktangles. All the recktangles have four coners and sides.

From: *How Many Rectangles?*

Models of teachers assessing children's understanding can be found in Cuisenaire's series of videotapes listed below.

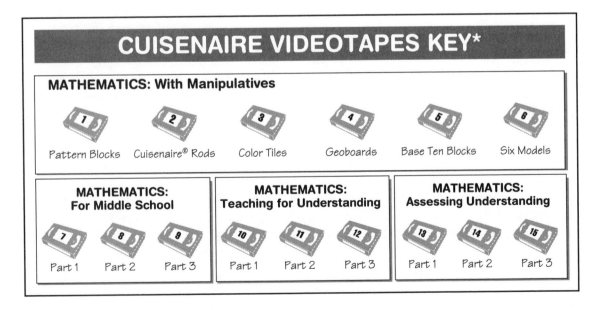

CUISENAIRE VIDEOTAPES KEY*

MATHEMATICS: With Manipulatives

1 Pattern Blocks	2 Cuisenaire® Rods	3 Color Tiles	4 Geoboards	5 Base Ten Blocks	6 Six Models

MATHEMATICS: For Middle School	**MATHEMATICS: Teaching for Understanding**	**MATHEMATICS: Assessing Understanding**
7 Part 1 8 Part 2 9 Part 3	10 Part 1 11 Part 2 12 Part 3	13 Part 1 14 Part 2 15 Part 3

*See *Overview of the Lessons*, pages 16–17, for specific lesson/video correlation.

Connect *the Super Source*™ to NCTM Standards.

	PROBLEM SOLVING	COMMUNICATION	REASONING	CONNECTIONS	Geometry	Logic	Measurement	Number	Patterns/Functions	Probability/Statistics
COUNTING COLORS	◆	◆	◆	◆						◆
CREATING PATTERNS	◆	◆	◆	◆					◆	
CREATURE FEATURES	◆	◆	◆	◆		◆		◆		
ESTIMATION JARS	◆	◆	◆	◆			◆	◆		
EXPLORATIONS WITH FOUR TILES	◆	◆	◆	◆		◆		◆		
FOLLOW ME!	◆	◆		◆				◆		
FRAMES OF TEN	◆		◆			◆		◆		
HALF AND HALF	◆		◆	◆	◆			◆		
HOW MANY RECTANGLES?	◆	◆	◆	◆		◆	◆	◆		
IT'S A FRAME-UP!	◆	◆	◆					◆	◆	
LAST SURVIVOR	◆	◆	◆					◆		
LINE UP FOUR	◆	◆		◆		◆		◆		
MIRROR, MIRROR ON THE WALL	◆	◆		◆	◆					
MYSTERY PATTERNS	◆	◆	◆	◆				◆		
SQUARE BY SQUARE	◆	◆	◆	◆		◆		◆		
VERY BUSY ANIMALS	◆	◆	◆					◆	◆	
WHAT'S IN THE BAG?	◆	◆	◆	◆				◆		
WHO'S GOT THE BIGGEST YARD?	◆	◆	◆	◆	◆		◆	◆		

Correlate *the Super Source*™ to your curriculum.

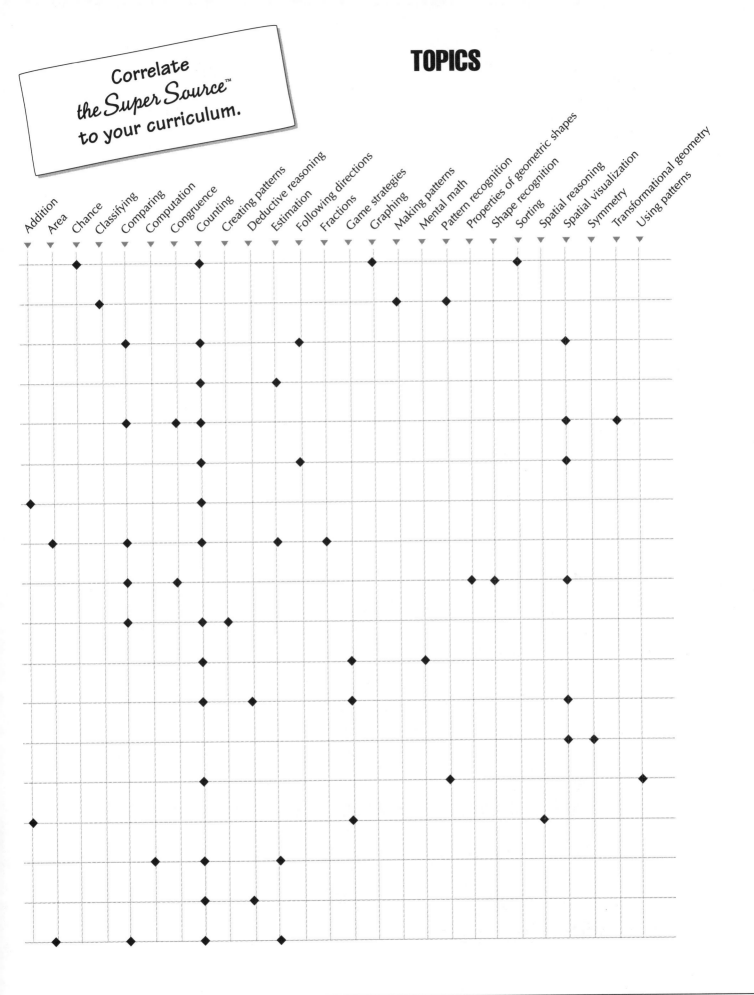

TOPICS

Addition	Area	Chance	Classifying	Comparing	Computation	Congruence	Counting	Creating patterns	Deductive reasoning	Estimation	Following directions	Fractions	Game strategies	Graphing	Making patterns	Mental math	Pattern recognition	Properties of geometric shapes	Shape recognition	Sorting	Spatial reasoning	Spatial visualization	Symmetry	Transformational geometry	Using patterns
		◆					◆							◆						◆					
			◆												◆		◆								
				◆			◆				◆											◆			
							◆			◆															
				◆		◆	◆															◆		◆	
							◆				◆											◆			
◆							◆																		
	◆			◆			◆			◆		◆													
				◆		◆												◆	◆			◆			
				◆			◆	◆																	
							◆						◆			◆									
							◆		◆				◆									◆			
																						◆	◆		
							◆										◆								◆
◆													◆								◆				
					◆		◆			◆															
							◆		◆																
	◆			◆			◆			◆															

More SUPER SOURCE™
at a glance:
COLOR TILES for Grades 3-4
and Grades 5-6

Classroom-tested activities contained in these *Super Source*™ Color Tiles books focus on the math strands in the charts below.

the Super Source™ Color Tiles, Grades 3-4

Geometry	Logic	Measurement
Number	Patterns/Functions	Probability/Statistics

the Super Source™ Color Tiles, Grades 5-6

Geometry	Logic	Measurement
Number	Patterns/Functions	Probability/Statistics

More SUPER SOURCE™
at a glance:
ADDITIONAL MANIPULATIVES
for Grades K-2

Classroom-tested activities contained in these *Super Source*™ books focus on the math strands as indicated in these charts.

...*the Super Source*™ Tangrams, Grades K-2

Geometry	Logic	Measurement
Number	Patterns/Functions	Probability/Statistics

...*the Super Source*™ Cuisenaire® Rods, Grades K-2

Geometry	Logic	Measurement
Number	Patterns/Functions	Probability/Statistics

...*the Super Source*™ Geoboards, Grades K-2

Geometry	Logic	Measurement
Number	Patterns/Functions	Probability/Statistics

...*the Super Source*™ Color Tiles, Grades K-2

Geometry	Logic	Measurement
Number	Patterns/Functions	Probability/Statistics

...*the Super Source*™ Pattern Blocks, Grades K-2

Geometry	Logic	Measurement
Number	Patterns/Functions	Probability/Statistics

Overview of the Lessons

See video key, page 11.

Color Tiles, Grades K-2

See video key, page 11.

COUNTING COLORS

- **Counting**
- **Sorting**
- **Graphing**
- **Chance**

Getting Ready

What You'll Need

Color Tiles, 10 of each color per pair

Counting Colors spinner, page 90

Paper clips, 1 per pair

Long sheets of paper

Overhead Color Tiles and/or Color Tile grid paper transparency (optional)

Overview

Children spin a spinner with sectors allocated to the four Color Tile colors and keep track of how many times each color comes up within a specific number of spins. In this activity, children have the opportunity to:

◆ organize and graph data

◆ determine the probability of the occurrence of unequally likely events

The Activity

Assemble a Counting Colors *spinner by first straightening the end of a paper clip and then pushing the endpoint through the center point of the spinner.*

Introducing

◆ Display the *Counting Colors* spinner. Invite children to describe what they see and how they might use the spinner.

◆ Draw these headings on the chalkboard and have children copy them on the top of long sheets of paper.

Green	Yellow	Blue	Red

◆ Call on a volunteer to spin the spinner. Have each child place a Color Tile on his or her paper in the column that corresponds to the color that comes up on the spinner.

◆ Choose more volunteers to spin the spinner. Continue having children record each spin by placing Color Tiles in the corresponding column on their papers.

◆ Elicit that by putting down tiles in this way, children have built a graph. Call on volunteers to "read" their graphs aloud.

On Their Own

Can you predict which color you will spin most often on this spinner?

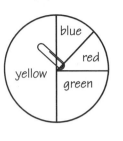

- Work with a partner. Share a spinner that looks like this one.

- Set up a graph by writing color names at the top of your paper this way.

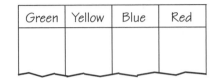

Green	Yellow	Blue	Red

- Get ready to spin the spinner. First decide which color you think will be the first to be spun 10 times. Write down your guess.

- Then take turns spinning the spinner. For each color that you spin, place a matching Color Tile in that column on the graph.

- Keep taking turns until 1 of the columns has 10 Color Tiles.

- Compare your guess to what happened. Be ready to talk about your graph.

The Bigger Picture

Thinking and Sharing

Invite pairs to post their graphs and report their results. Then compile everyone's findings into a larger class graph.

Use prompts such as these to promote class discussion:

- ◆ What did you notice about your results?

- ◆ Whose guesses turned out to be correct? Why did you guess that color?

- ◆ What does the class graph show about the Color Tile with the most spins?

- ◆ How does the class graph compare to your own graph?

- ◆ Would you call the spinner a "fair" spinner? Explain.

Extending the Activity

Have children create a new face for their spinner using any three Color Tiles and any allotment of sector space they like. Then have them repeat the activity.

Where's the Mathematics?

This activity introduces children to topics in probability. It also provides children with an opportunity to make connections among various areas of mathematics as they use counting and comparing skills to make their graphs and to work intuitively with fractions.

Many children are familiar with the use of spinners as part of board games that they have played at home. Typically, such spinners are divided into equal sectors and offer a "fair chance, or equally likely chances," of stopping on any given sector. Having a "fair chance" is what makes the game fun to play.

The spinner used in this activity is not fair. The chances of the spinner stopping on yellow are twice as great as its stopping on green and four times greater than its stopping on blue or red. Many children will not recognize this fact just by looking at the spinner. They will have to work through this activity and then, during the class discussion, reflect on why so many of their classmates' graphs had more yellow Color Tiles than green, blue, or red.

When children are initially asked to predict which color they will spin the most, many will pick their favorite color without observing the effect that the relative sizes of the sectors might have on the outcome. In fact, if you were to repeat this activity several days or weeks later, some children would still predict their favorite color. Only frequent experience with chance events over time can help children to solidify their grasp of probability.

Although the "unfair" spinner makes the lesson focus on chance events, children also get needed practice in collecting, organizing, and analyzing data. Young children gain experience with concrete graphs as they touch and manipulate actual objects. Watching how the pooling of information creates one large class graph that mimics the shape of many of the individual graphs can be an interesting revelation to children.

Later, as they become more sophisticated, children can move to more representational or abstract graphing.

In this activity, children have the opportunity to work with both experimental and theoretical probability. *Experimental probability* is the probability of an event based on the results of an actual experiment. Children experiment as they use the spinners and collect their data. During the first four spins, children might spin blue, green, yellow, and red, in which case the experimental probability of spinning a yellow is one out of four, or 1/4. *Theoretical probability* is what is likely to happen based on a great deal of data. When the children pool their collective data, make one large classroom graph, and analyze it, they are moving toward determining theoretical probability. For the spinner used in this activity, the theoretical probability of landing on yellow is one out of two, or 1/2, because the yellow sector is one half of the whole spinner. Theoretically, if the spinner were spun four times, one would expect the spinner to land on yellow twice. Frequently, the experimental probability of just a few spins does not exactly match the theoretical probability one would predict as the outcome. In later grades, children learn that the theoretical probability of spinning one color over another is based on the assumption that the spinner has been spun hundreds, or even thousands, of times.

Theoretically, then, half the spins will produce a tile in the yellow column. But the question is not "Which color will be spun the most?" but "Which color will be the first to be spun 10 times?" As it happens, the theoretical probability that yellow will be the first color to reach 10 spins is much more than half; in theory, yellow will win about 93% of the time and green about 6.5% of the time. Children's responses may not reflect this figure, though, because 12 experiments is still a small sample space. Repeating the activity over time and continuing to add the results to the original class graph will give results that will more closely align with what is theoretically probable.

CREATING PATTERNS

- **Making patterns**
- **Pattern recognition**
- **Sorting and classifying**
- **Graphing**

Getting Ready

What You'll Need

Color Tiles, about 40 per child

Color Tile grid paper cut and taped into 1" x 10" strips, 1 strip per child, page 102

Crayons

Overhead Color Tiles and/or Color Tile grid paper transparency (optional)

Overview

Children use Color Tiles to create repeating patterns. Then they sort and classify their patterns and organize them into a graph. In this activity, children have the opportunity to:

- ◆ notice ways in which some patterns are different from one another

- ◆ notice ways in which some patterns are like others

- ◆ organize and analyze information on a graph

The Activity

Introducing

- ◆ Line up several children to form a boy-girl-boy-girl pattern. Ask other children to tell who might come next in the pattern.

- ◆ Then have other children line up, alternately standing and kneeling. Ask a volunteer to suggest what the next child in the pattern should be doing.

- ◆ Repeat with children alternately facing backward and facing forward.

- ◆ Point out that the boy-girl, standing-kneeling, backward-forward patterns were all alike in some way. Ask why this is so.

- ◆ Establish that in each pattern, just two things kept alternating. Explain that an easy way to describe a pattern that has only two different parts is by using the letters *AB*, in which each letter stands for a different part.

- ◆ Have boys and girls line up in *ABB, ABA,* and *AAB* patterns. Discuss how the letters represent the patterns.

On Their Own

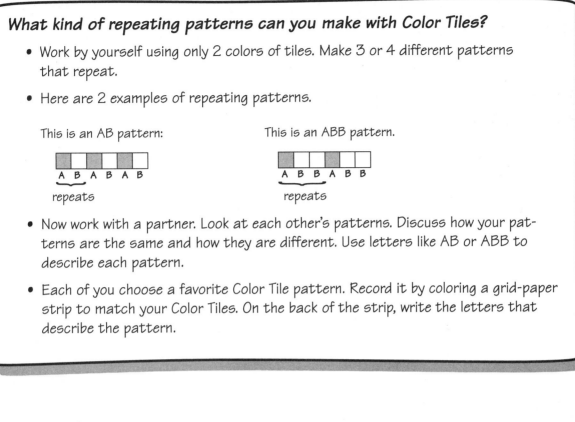

What kind of repeating patterns can you make with Color Tiles?

- Work by yourself using only 2 colors of tiles. Make 3 or 4 different patterns that repeat.

- Here are 2 examples of repeating patterns.

This is an AB pattern:

A B A B A B

repeats

This is an ABB pattern.

A B B A B B

repeats

- Now work with a partner. Look at each other's patterns. Discuss how your patterns are the same and how they are different. Use letters like AB or ABB to describe each pattern.

- Each of you choose a favorite Color Tile pattern. Record it by coloring a grid-paper strip to match your Color Tiles. On the back of the strip, write the letters that describe the pattern.

The Bigger Picture

Thinking and Sharing

Invite one child to post a recording on the chalkboard. Help the child to identify the pattern and the way in which the colors repeat by using combinations of the letters A and B. Write the letters above the posting. Call on other children to post patterns that are the same, each below the next, to form a column.

Have a volunteer display a pattern that is different from those already posted. Create a new column for this pattern by having the child post it then write identifying letters above it. Continue in this way, creating additional columns, as needed, until all children's recordings are in one or another column of the class graph.

Use prompts like these to promote class discussion:

- How are the postings in each column of the graph alike? How are they different?

- What kind of pattern did most children make? What kind did fewest children make?

- (Point to any pattern.) How many of each color would you use to add four more Color Tiles to this pattern? to add six more tiles? eight more tiles?

- Does looking at the graph give you any new ideas for Color Tile patterns? If so, describe them.

Extending the Activity

Have children make and name two different patterns using Color Tiles in three or four colors.

<table><tr><td>**Teacher Talk**</td></tr></table>

Where's the Mathematics?

Even if children simply imitate the patterns given in the examples—*AB* and *ABB*—the different colors they use will suggest that there is a lot of data that can be sorted and classified according to the similarities and differences children perceive.

In the course of the activity, children work from a specific case (their individual patterns) to a general case as they compare their individual patterns with those of their classmates and identify elements that their patterns have in common. Using just two colors, children could theoretically make twelve different *AB* patterns. (A similar kind of listing would show that there are twelve different *ABB* patterns).

red-blue	red-green	red-yellow
blue-red	blue-green	blue-yellow
green-red	green-blue	green-yellow
yellow-red	yellow-blue	yellow-green

It may take children some time to come to terms with the fact that all the above are *AB* patterns—especially if, for reasons of their own, they rejected a red-blue pattern for a blue-red pattern in their individual work. However, once they do recognize and understand what an *AB* pattern is, the stage is set for them to look critically at other patterns and look for unifying or descriptive rules.

If children choose *AB* patterns as their favorites, they can record the patterns on ten-square strips of paper so that they just fit; that is, so that there are five repeats of the pattern. However, if they choose a three-tile pattern such as *ABB*, their recording will either have one square uncolored or they will fill

---

up the strip by coloring in the tenth square with the A color, as shown by the following diagrams.

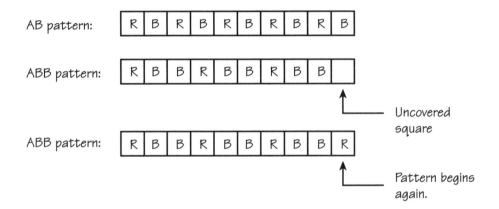

AB pattern:

ABB pattern:

— Uncovered square

ABB pattern:

— Pattern begins again.

The three scenarios above expose children in a very informal way to the concepts of division and divisibility. The first shows that two is a divisor of ten since the ten squares can be completely covered by groups of two with no remainders. The second shows that three is not a divisor of ten since the ten squares can be covered only by three groups of three with one square left uncovered, the "remainder." Likewise, the third shows that three is not a divisor of ten, and that the tenth square may be covered by one of the three tiles in the pattern (or that the tenth square is one third of the pattern: $10 \div 3 = 3\frac{1}{3}$).

Once the patterns are posted, children can examine them and predict what colors the next tile(s) would be. The posted work also provides children with opportunities to develop ideas for even more complex pattern schemes, such as *ABBA*, *AAAB*, and *AABBAB*.

CREATURE FEATURES

- Spatial visualization
- Following directions
- Counting
- Comparing

Getting Ready

What You'll Need

Color Tiles, 30 per child

Construction paper (white), 1 large sheet per child

Colored paper cut into 1" squares to match Color Tiles

Glue stick or tape

Crayons

Creature Features worksheet, page 91

Overhead Color Tiles and/or Color Tile grid paper transparency (optional)

Overview

Children use several Color Tiles to make a "creature." They write descriptions of their creatures, then try to match one another's creatures to the descriptions. In this activity, children have an opportunity to:

- ◆ identify attributes of a Color Tile design
- ◆ communicate specific information
- ◆ solve a problem by listening to numerical and verbal clues

The Activity

Introducing

- ◆ Build and display this Color Tile "creature."
- ◆ On the chalkboard, make a replica of the *Creature Features* worksheet.
- ◆ Introduce your creature as Zork, and write this name in the blank to complete the first sentence on the board.
- ◆ Ask children to help you fill in more information about Zork. Call on volunteers to give the number of tiles of each color used to make Zork.
- ◆ Elicit other facts about Zork and record them. Children might suggest some physical details such as, "Zork's legs are green," or "Zork's antennae are up in the air."

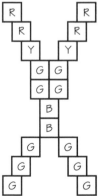

On Their Own

Can you match a Color Tile mystery creature to its description?

- Put 20 to 30 Color Tiles on a piece of construction paper.
- Move the tiles around on the paper to make a mystery creature that you like. Keep your creature a secret.
- Now take 1 tile away. Glue a matching paper square in its place. Do the same for each of the other tiles.
- Use crayons to draw parts on your creature, such as eyes and ears.
- Name your creature. Then, on your Creature Features worksheet, record your creature's name, how many tiles you used to make it, and other facts about it.
  For example: My creature has no arms.
  It has green legs.
  It has 2 antennae.
- Put your mystery creature facedown in the middle of a table. Your other group members should do the same. Mix up the papers. Then turn them faceup.
- Take turns reading aloud what you wrote about your creatures. Work together to find the creature that matches each description.
- Choose 1 of your group's creatures. Be ready to discuss it with the class.

The Bigger Picture

Thinking and Sharing

Post the creatures that each group chose. Invite a volunteer from one of the groups to share the description of that group's posted creature. Caution other group members not to give the secret away while the rest of the class tries to guess which mystery creature matches each description.

Use prompts like these to promote class discussion:

- What information helped you the most to identify a posted mystery creature?
- What is another clue that would describe this creature? (Point to one.)
- How are any two creatures the same? How are they different?
- Which creature(s) was (were) made from the fewest tiles? the most tiles?

Extending the Activity

1. Have children help you to create a class graph of the mystery creatures by sorting the creatures according to how many tiles were used to make them.

2. Have pairs of children work together using fifty tiles to make a giant creature.

Where's the Mathematics?

This activity gives children a chance to use their imagination. Transferring the creature to paper by replacing each tile with a colored paper square helps children with their visual and spatial relationships. Counting and writing skills are called into play when children use numbers and words to convey information that will enable other children to correctly identify the creature. As children listen to the clues read to them, they have a chance to use deductive reasoning. They do this by sorting through many different pictures, eliminating the ones that do not match the clues, then zeroing in on the creature that fulfills all the clues.

Children quickly learn that being told the total number of Color Tiles in a creature is not particularly helpful because it is hard to quickly count up to a number between 20 and 30. Being told the numbers of the various colors of tiles would be more helpful. Hearing that a creature has 4 red tiles automatically eliminates many of the drawings, but most likely there will still be a few that feature 4 red tiles, so children need more clues. At this point, the task gets easier, because there is a smaller pool of drawings to consider. Younger children may find it helpful for one child to read a few clues, move the pictures that fit those clues to an area apart from the rest of the pictures, and then continue to read the rest of the clues.

Because two creatures may have exactly the same color breakdown, children need to listen to other information about the creature to help them find the exact one being described. These additional facts must refer to the physical qualities of the creature being described. If necessary, children can be guided to see that facts such as "Zork eats worms and baby bats for breakfast" are creative, but not very helpful because they do not describe Zork's physical appearance.

In the chart below, various kinds of facts are listed for one child's mystery creature named Botto.

Facts about Botto.
1. Botto has two legs.
2. Botto's legs are very strong.
3. Botto has red ears.
4. Botto's ears can hear a sound ten miles away.

Notice that facts 1 and 3 describe Botto's physical appearance, and would therefore be more helpful in identifying Botto than would facts 2 and 4.

Botto

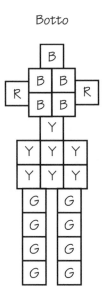

This activity encourages children to be accurate. If the writer of the facts has counted the Color Tiles incorrectly, the facts might confuse, rather than help, the listener. Asking children to describe how two creatures are different hones children's visual discrimination skills. Asking them to look for features that make their creatures alike prepares children to reason inductively and make generalizations.

ESTIMATION JARS

Getting Ready

What You'll Need

Color Tiles, about 30 per pair

Plastic containers of different sizes, 3 per pair

Rubber bands, 3 per pair

Overview

Children estimate, then count, the numbers of Color Tiles that will fill a variety of containers. In this activity, children have the opportunity to:

◆ make and revise estimates

◆ use the concepts of grouping and place value

The Activity

In On Their Own, *offer the choice of counting beyond ones only to children who are ready for this.*

Introducing

◆ Hold up a container filled to the top with Color Tiles. Ask children how many tiles they think are in the container. List children's names and guesses, each time asking children to explain why their guesses, or estimates, make sense.

◆ Begin counting the contents of the container aloud. Halfway through, ask children whether they would like to change their estimates and, if so, why. Record children's new estimates next to their original ones.

◆ Finish counting the tiles and invite children to compare their estimates with the actual number of tiles.

On Their Own

Can you estimate how many Color Tiles are in a container?

- Work with a partner. Take a plastic container. Put a rubber band around the halfway point.

- Fill the container to the top with Color Tiles.

- Each of you makes your best guess, or estimate, of how many tiles the container holds. Record your estimates.

- Now check your estimates by counting the tiles.
  - First, spill out about *half* the tiles.
  - Then decide how you will count them—by 1s, 2s, 5s, or 10s. Stack the tiles in groups of that number. (If you will count by 1s, each pile should have 1 tile.)

- When you have counted about half the tiles, look at your estimate. If you want to change it, record your second estimate next to your first.

- Now count all the tiles. Record the number next to your estimates and draw a box around it.

- Repeat the activity with 2 different containers.

- Be ready to talk about how you made your estimates.

The Bigger Picture

Thinking and Sharing

Have children talk about what happened as they worked through the activity.

Use prompts such as these to promote class discussion:

- How did you make your first estimate?

- Did you change your estimate after you counted half the tiles? Why or why not?

- How did you count? What do you think was the most helpful way to count? Why do you think so?

- Was it easier to estimate when you worked with the second or third container? Explain.

Extending the Activity

Have children repeat the activity using Snap™ Cubes instead of Color Tiles.

Where's the Mathematics?

Activities involving estimation help young children to develop good number sense and prepare them to think about whether their answers are reasonable or not. Children must learn that an estimate is not just a wild guess. Having children count to check their guesses for about half the Color Tiles and allowing them to revise their estimates if they want to will help children learn that estimates are related to prior knowledge and to benchmarks. Having children share the strategies that they used for making their estimates also helps educate other children to the nature of estimates.

When asked for their initial estimate, some young children may look at the container and think, "It looks pretty big so I'll name a big number like 1,000." Then, as they count about half the tiles and find there are 46, which is no where near 1,000 they should realize that their first guess was not a good one. Children may now reason, "I have about as much room left to go as I have already filled. That means that I can probably put another 46 tiles in the container." At this point, children may simply conclude that the container holds about 46 + 46, or 92, tiles. Those who feel comfortable with the idea of estimating may use rounding in an informal way to arrive at an estimate more quickly. Some children may reason, "Since 46 is almost 50, about 50 + 50, or 100, should fill the container." Eventually, children may generalize that they can double the number they get after counting halfway.

Children may use what they already know about the number of tiles they counted in one container to estimate the number in another. Their success in doing so will indicate how well they can judge the relative sizes of the container. For example, if children have determined that the first container

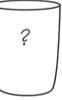

100 tiles

?

below holds 100 tiles, they may estimate that the second container holds more—perhaps twice as many—simply because it is about twice as tall as the first. Children who also take into consideration that the second container is about half as wide as the first may decide that these two changes in dimensions cancel each other out and estimate that the second container holds about the same amount as the first. (In fact, if both shapes are cylinders and the second is twice as tall but half as wide as the first, the second should hold about half as many tiles as the first.) In using what they know about the tile capacity of one container to estimate the tile capacity of another, children use spatial reasoning as they are informally exposed to the idea of volume.

At first, some children may not understand that an estimate is an inexact answer. They may think that if they estimate 44 and the actual count is 41, then their estimate is wrong. Teaching children to phrase their estimates as "about 40" and later, when they have become more proficient at making estimates, as "between 40 and 45," is likely to encourage them to be risk-takers, willing to make an educated guess.

Children can also come to appreciate the inexactness of an estimate when they compare the number of tiles different pairs of children were able to pack into the same container. Some children may pack the Color Tiles as neatly and closely as possible; others may just spill a handful of Color Tiles into the container. Even if two pairs of children use the same method for putting their tiles into the container, their final answers are apt to come out close together without being exactly the same.

EXPLORATIONS WITH FOUR TILES

- Comparing
- Counting
- Transformational geometry
- Congruence
- Spatial visualization

Getting Ready

What You'll Need

Color Tiles, 4 of 1 color per child

Color Tile grid paper, 1 sheet per child, page 102

Overhead Color Tiles and/or Color Tile grid paper transparency (optional)

Overview

Children try to make all the different shapes that can be made by putting together four Color Tiles so that at least one full side of each tile touches a full side of another tile. In this activity, children have the opportunity to:

- ◆ use spatial visualization to build shapes
- ◆ develop strategies for finding new shapes
- ◆ test to find shapes that are flips or turns of other shapes

The Activity

Introducing

- ◆ Display this Color Tile shape and have children copy it.
- ◆ Ask children to tell something about the shape. Establish that it is made up of three Color Tiles and that every tile shares at least one complete side with another tile.
- ◆ Ask children to find another way to arrange the three tiles so that every tile touches at least one complete side of another tile.
- ◆ Have volunteers who think they have found different shapes display them.
- ◆ Model how to record the first shape on grid paper and cut it out. Then have children record and cut out their shapes.
- ◆ Collect the cutout shapes, making two piles, one for each of the two possible arrangements. Show how, by flipping or turning the pieces in each pile, you can fit them over each other exactly to make a neat stack.

On Their Own

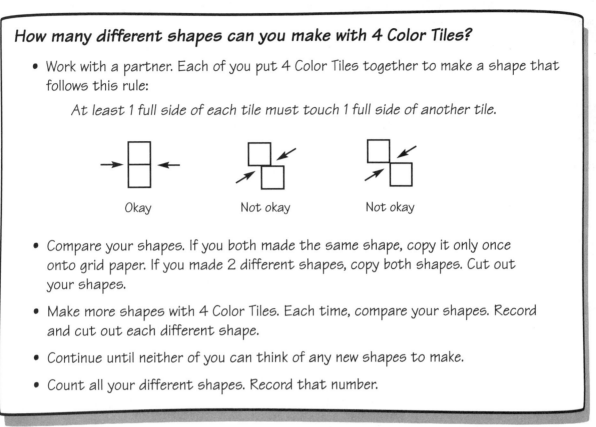

How many different shapes can you make with 4 Color Tiles?

- Work with a partner. Each of you put 4 Color Tiles together to make a shape that follows this rule:

    At least 1 full side of each tile must touch 1 full side of another tile.

    Okay   Not okay   Not okay

- Compare your shapes. If you both made the same shape, copy it only once onto grid paper. If you made 2 different shapes, copy both shapes. Cut out your shapes.

- Make more shapes with 4 Color Tiles. Each time, compare your shapes. Record and cut out each different shape.

- Continue until neither of you can think of any new shapes to make.

- Count all your different shapes. Record that number.

The Bigger Picture

Thinking and Sharing

Ask a volunteer to tape one of the shapes to the chalkboard. Call on other volunteers, one at a time, to post different shapes. As children bring up shapes, have them test each new shape against those already posted, flipping and/or turning them, to make sure theirs is unique.

Use prompts such as these to promote class discussion:

- How did you and your partner decide whether or not your shapes were different?

- Did you use any of your old shapes to find new ones? If so, how did you do this?

- How did you know that you found all of the different shapes?

- How many different shapes are there?

Extending the Activity

1. Have children arrange their five unique shapes like a jigsaw puzzle on a piece of construction paper so that the sides of the pieces touch and no spaces are left between them.

2. Have children investigate all the possible shapes that can be made with different arrangements of five Color Tiles.

Where's the Mathematics?

In this activity, children are given a hands-on introduction to transformational geometry. As children create shapes with four squares, then move the basic squares around to create new shapes, the idea of transformation becomes concrete.

There are five possible shapes that can be made by arranging four squares so that at least one complete side of each square touches a complete side of another square.

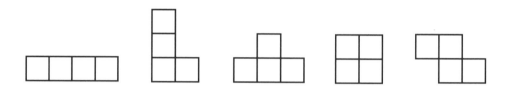

In the process of creating unique shapes and eliminating duplicates, some children may simply try to visualize two Color Tile shapes in different positions. Other children may compare two shapes by actually turning one of their shapes before they record a new shape. Still others may cut out their paper shapes, then turn and flip them to see whether or not they match any other shapes.

As children discuss their strategies for determining whether or not two shapes are the same, you may want to informally introduce the terms *turning, flipping,* and *sliding*—terms used in transformational geometry.

Turning shape B, below, a quarter turn clockwise until it is oriented the same way as shape A makes it easy to see that the two shapes are identical.

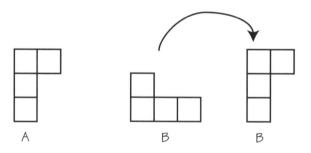

A   B   B

Flipping is a term used to describe picking up a figure and turning it over, as shown on the next page. Many children in grades K-2 are likely to have difficulty imagining what a Color Tile shape would look like if it were flipped over. Thus, it is probably best to use the paper shapes to demonstrate flipping.

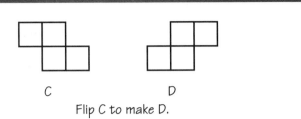

C   D

Flip C to make D.

Depending on the orientation of the original figure, children may observe that a turn *or* a flip may result in the same shape.

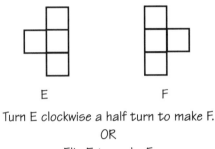

E   F

Turn E clockwise a half turn to make F.
OR
Flip E to make F.

Sliding describes the movement of a shape from one place in a plane to another while maintaining its original orientation.

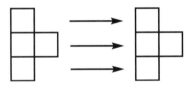

Asking children to describe how they can turn, flip, and/or slide a cutout shape so that it will exactly match another child's shape will contribute to children's spatial reasoning ability and their understanding of congruence.

During *On Their Own*, children may ask you if they have found all the possible shapes that can be made with four squares. Encourage children to work to find all the possible shapes themselves (although it is not necessary that each group do so). Later, during the class discussion, some children may find it helpful to hear others describe their process of searching for unique shapes. For example, a child might describe starting with the shape that has all four squares in a row, then leaving three of the squares and moving just the fourth square to find all the positions in which it could be placed to create new shapes. Another child might then tell of leaving only two of the squares in a row and moving the other two squares around until all those possibilities have been exhausted.

FOLLOW ME!

Getting Ready

What You'll Need

Color Tiles, 12 per pair

Large books or boxes to use as barriers

Overhead Color Tiles and/or Color Tile grid paper transparency (optional)

Overview

Children take turns building a secret Color Tile design and try to build their partner's design from clues their partner gives them. In this activity, children have the opportunity to:

◆ identify attributes of geometric shapes

◆ communicate specific information

◆ use spatial vocabulary

The Activity

Adjust the number of tiles so that your children are suitably challenged.

Introducing

◆ Use Color Tiles to make a design like the one shown and keep it hidden. Tell children you want them to listen to clues about this shape.

B	B
R	Y

◆ Now give one descriptive clue about your design. For example, you might say, "I used four tiles." Then ask children to try to make your design with Color Tiles.

◆ Observe children's work. Remark that you see many designs that follow your clue but none that are exactly like yours. Invite children to speculate about why this might be.

◆ Give another clue, for example, "My tiles form a big square." Allow time for children to rearrange their designs to fit this second clue. Again, move around the room and comment that the second clue seems to have been helpful. Ask what additional information children might need to make your design exactly.

◆ One at a time, give clues such as, "The top two tiles are blue," "The bottom right tile is yellow," and "The bottom left tile is red." Let children change their designs to fit each new clue until their designs match yours. Then reveal your design.

On Their Own

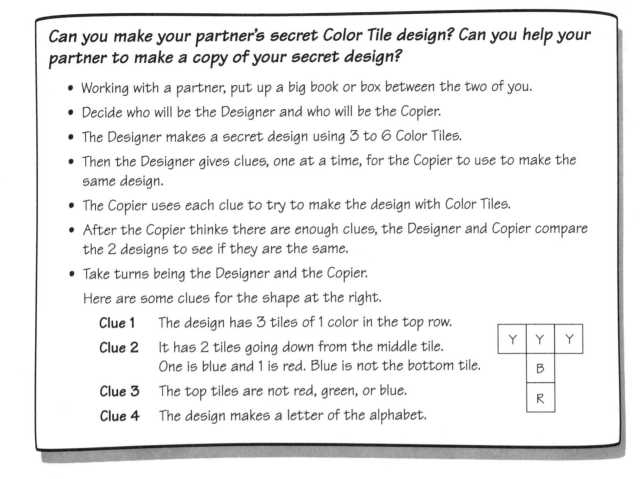

Can you make your partner's secret Color Tile design? Can you help your partner to make a copy of your secret design?

- Working with a partner, put up a big book or box between the two of you.

- Decide who will be the Designer and who will be the Copier.

- The Designer makes a secret design using 3 to 6 Color Tiles.

- Then the Designer gives clues, one at a time, for the Copier to use to make the same design.

- The Copier uses each clue to try to make the design with Color Tiles.

- After the Copier thinks there are enough clues, the Designer and Copier compare the 2 designs to see if they are the same.

- Take turns being the Designer and the Copier.

  Here are some clues for the shape at the right.

  Clue 1   The design has 3 tiles of 1 color in the top row.

  Clue 2   It has 2 tiles going down from the middle tile.
  One is blue and 1 is red. Blue is not the bottom tile.

  Clue 3   The top tiles are not red, green, or blue.

  Clue 4   The design makes a letter of the alphabet.

The Bigger Picture

Thinking and Sharing

Invite pairs to discuss their experiences both describing designs and following directions. Have some pairs draw their last design on the chalkboard.

Use prompts like these to promote class discussion:

- ◆ What was difficult about this activity? What was easy?

- ◆ What are some of the directions you used to describe the way the tiles in your design were placed?

- ◆ Were some shapes easier to copy than others? Why?

- ◆ What kinds of clues were the most helpful?

- ◆ How could you describe how the tiles in the designs drawn on the chalkboard are arranged?

Extending the Activity

1. Have children make and copy more complex designs.

2. Present children with the same challenge using Snap™ Cubes or Pattern Blocks.

Where's the Mathematics?

Communicating mathematically is an important skill in building mathematical understanding. This activity provides young children with practice in using precise language to build geometric shapes. Creating a good set of directions requires spatial terms such as *left*, *right*, *under*, *above*, *horizontal*, *vertical*, and *diagonal*; numerical terms such as *first*, *third*, and *ten*; and descriptive words, such as *red*, *blue*, *green*, and *yellow*. Doing an activity that demands this kind of vocabulary helps children to make words such as these a natural part of their language. This is not a competitive game. Children should recognize that the goal of the Designer is not to try to trick the Copier but rather to provide useful descriptions that enable the Copier to build an exact replica of the design.

The importance of the skills brought to the task by both partners— describing, listening, visualizing, and questioning—becomes more and more evident as children repeat the activity and take turns at the two roles.

When communicating, young children may use body language as well as verbal language. For instance, instead of saying "right," a child might say, "Put two tiles on this side" and wave his or her right hand in the air to indicate what is meant by "this side." (If children are sitting across from each other, rather than side-by-side, this use of body language may actually lead to the Copier putting the two tiles on the left rather than the right because the Copier followed the visual cue, which was a hand waving on the Copier's left side.)

In comparing the design and its copy, children have an opportunity to deepen their understanding of the word *identical*. Children may need to scrutinize their designs carefully to determine whether or not they really match their partner's design in every way. For example, here are two designs that are congruent. However, since the design on the left has to be flipped to look exactly like the design on the right, they are not identical.

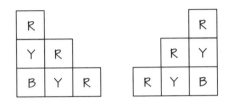

By comparing designs, partners get feedback on how well they were able to communicate with each other. Children should be encouraged to try to figure out which parts of the descriptions may have been misinterpreted and to discuss better ways of explaining or describing those particular attributes of the designs.

Language development is also closely tied to mathematical thinking. Children need to develop skills in both receptive and expressive language. By having the opportunity to give and receive clues, both areas of language development are emphasized. Because these skills are in a constant state of development, you can use this activity over and over again to assess growth in vocabulary and interpreting skills. You can also use it after you have modeled vocabulary to see what progress has been made.

FRAMES OF TEN

Getting Ready

What You'll Need

Color Tiles, 30 each of 2 different colors per pair

Frames of Ten outlines, 2 sheets per pair, page 92

Crayons

Overhead Color Tiles and/or Color Tile grid paper transparency (optional)

Overview

Children construct two-color rectangular frames of ten Color Tiles. Then they write number sentences that describe their frames. In this activity, children have an opportunity to:

◆ see concrete representations of sums of ten

◆ practice writing number sentences

◆ create and analyze a graph

The Activity

Introducing

◆ On a piece of paper, construct and display a frame using twelve Color Tiles in two different colors, as shown.

◆ Ask children how many tiles of each color make up the frame. Then ask them to suggest a number sentence that uses these numbers and whose sum is twelve.

◆ Elicit that both $8 + 4 = 12$ and $4 + 8 = 12$ describe the colors in the frame. Write one of these inside the frame.

◆ Repeat this process twice more, again using twelve tiles of two colors to show pairs of addends whose sum is twelve. Ask children to describe each frame using number sentences. Here are some examples:

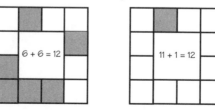

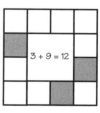

On Their Own

- Work with a partner. Use only 2 colors of tiles to make as many different frames of 10 tiles as you can. Put each frame on an outline like this one:

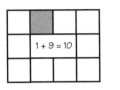

- Record your frames by coloring the squares to match the colors of your tiles. Inside each frame, write a number sentence that tells the number of tiles of each color and the sum. Here is an example of how a frame with 1 green tile and 9 yellow tiles would look:

1 + 9 = 10

- When you have made as many different frames as you can, cut them out.

The Bigger Picture

Thinking and Sharing

Invite one pair to post one of their frames and read aloud their number sentence. Have children write the addends below the frame. Ask other children with the same frame to post theirs in the same column. Follow the same procedure until all the different frames and pairs of addends have been posted to create a graph.

Use prompts like these to promote class discussion:

- How many different frames did you and your partner find?

- What do you notice when you look at the graph?

- Do all the frames with the same number sentence look alike? Why or why not?

- Which posted number sentence has the most frames? the fewest frames?

- How many more children made a frame for ———— than for ————?

- Is there anything else you notice about this graph?

- Are there any other possible number sentences whose sum is ten? How do you know?

Writing

Have children make any shape using ten tiles of two colors. Ask children to copy the shape onto paper and write a number sentence for it.

Extending the Activity

1. Have children make frames with another number of tiles, such as 14, 16, or 20.

2. Have children make frames of ten using three or four colors. Ask them to write these longer number sentences under the frames.

Where's the Mathematics?

The number ten is pivotal in our base-ten system of numeration, and children benefit from many opportunities to work with the addends of ten. The activity in *On Their Own* generates many examples of how the number ten can be broken down into two smaller numbers. The class graphing activity will pull this multitude of examples into a simple graph with only five columns, thus identifying the common mathematical patterns uniting all of the frames of ten that the children just created.

The question of whether number sentences such as 8 + 2 = 10 and 2 + 8 = 10 should be graphed in the same column is likely to arise during the class discussion. Looking over their work, children will probably notice that some children have made frames of two yellow and eight blue tiles and written 2 + 8 = 10, whereas other children have made frames also using two yellow and eight blue but have written 8 + 2 = 10. Children thus are apt to realize that the order of the addends does not matter. Later, children learn that this reversal of the addends in an addition problem is formally called the *commutative property of addition*. Internalizing this idea means that children have half as many addition facts to learn.

Creating a graph from data that the children themselves have created is a good way to see how graphs can help to analyze a lot of information by organizing it into just a few columns.

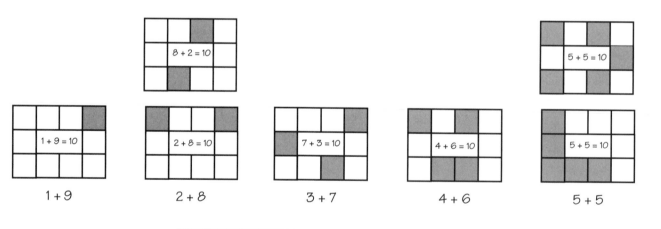

Children sort their frames and find commonalities in order to create the graph. They must look beyond colors to find what two frames have in common. For example, one child used two red and eight blue tiles, whereas another child used eight green and two yellow. When looking only at colors, these frames might seem very different, but the number sentences provide a link that places both of these frames in the same column. Likewise, two children may have used two red and eight blue tiles but placed them differently on their frames. Again, the number sentences link the two frames and override the issue of the different color placements.

To answer, "How many more children made a frame for ———— than for ————?", some children will count all of the data in each column and then subtract the two numbers. Other children will take a more visual approach to this question, comparing the heights of the two columns and counting only the data that makes the taller column tower above the shorter one. An open-ended question such as "Is there anything else you notice about this graph?" allows children to make observations that you may never even have considered when you gave children this activity.

Since children were directed to use two different colors when making their frames, the number sentence $0 + 10 = 10$ will probably not be suggested. However, you can call children's attention to $0 + 10 = 10$ and ask them to explain what this number sentence would look like when children build their frames from colored tiles. After a little thought, children will probably respond that this means that the frame has ten tiles, all of the same color.

HALF AND HALF

- Counting
- Comparing
- Estimation
- Area
- Fractions

Getting Ready

What You'll Need

Color Tiles, 12 of 1 color and 12 of another color per pair

Half and Half outlines, 1 set per pair, pages 93-94

Crayons

Overhead Color Tiles and/or Color Tile grid paper transparency (optional)

The Activity

Overview

Children predict whether or not the outlines of various shapes can be filled with an equal number of Color Tiles of two different colors. They use Color Tiles to check their predictions, then create addition sentences to describe their results. In this activity, children have the opportunity to:

- ◆ predict and count
- ◆ discover that there are many ways to show one half
- ◆ explore how the concept of one half is linked to various arithmetic operations

Introducing

- ◆ Display this shape consisting of two yellow and two blue Color Tiles.
- ◆ Ask children to tell what fraction of the shape is yellow and what fraction is blue. Have them explain why they think as they do.
- ◆ Determine that the shape is half yellow and half blue because the number of yellow tiles is equal to the number of blue tiles. Tell children that a number sentence that could be used to describe the tiles in this shape is $2 + 2 = 4$.
- ◆ Display these shapes. Establish that, even though the position of the tiles in these shapes differ, since they all have an equal number of yellow and blue tiles, they can all be described with the number sentence $2 + 2 = 4$.
- ◆ Arrange three yellow and two blue Color Tiles, and ask whether this shape is half yellow and half blue.
- ◆ Establish that the shape does not show halves because there are more yellow tiles than blue tiles. Elicit that a number sentence to describe the tiles in the shape could be $3 + 2 = 5$.

On Their Own

Which of these shapes can be covered with Color Tiles so that half of the shape is 1 color and half is another color?

- Work with a partner. Each of you choose a different Color Tile and gather 12 tiles of that color. You will need shape outlines that look like these:

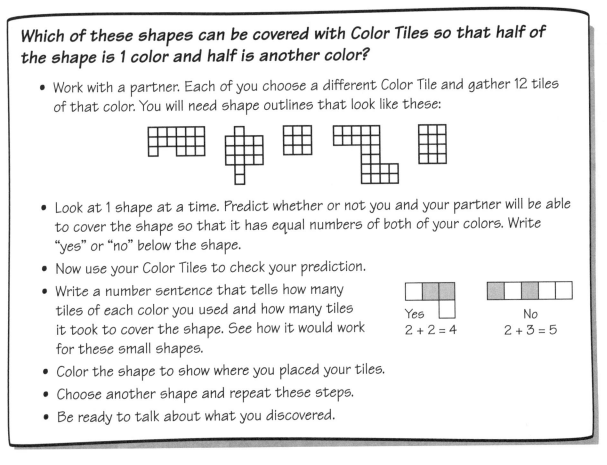

- Look at 1 shape at a time. Predict whether or not you and your partner will be able to cover the shape so that it has equal numbers of both of your colors. Write "yes" or "no" below the shape.
- Now use your Color Tiles to check your prediction.
- Write a number sentence that tells how many tiles of each color you used and how many tiles it took to cover the shape. See how it would work for these small shapes.

    Yes
    2 + 2 = 4

    No
    2 + 3 = 5

- Color the shape to show where you placed your tiles.
- Choose another shape and repeat these steps.
- Be ready to talk about what you discovered.

The Bigger Picture

Thinking and Sharing

Invite pairs of children to share and compare their results and their strategies.

Use prompts like these to promote class discussion:

- Can you tell just from looking at a shape whether you will be able to cover it equally with tiles of two different colors? If so, how?
- How did you check to see if you had "half and half?"
- As you worked, did you change strategies for predicting or checking? If so, tell what you did.
- What did you notice about the addition sentences that described the different results?

Extending the Activity

1. Have children make their own shapes on 1-inch grid paper for other children to check to see whether they can be covered with the same number of tiles of each of two colors.

2. Create shapes without the grid lines and challenge children to predict whether or not the shapes can be covered "half and half" with Color Tiles.

3. Ask children to try to cover shapes with equal numbers of three different colors of tiles.

Where's the Mathematics?

The task of determining whether or not a shape can be filled equally with tiles of two colors connects many mathematical concepts. Finding half of a number is the same as dividing that number by two. Seeing that a shape that contains ten squares that can be covered with five red tiles and five yellow tiles is another way of saying that ten squares may be divided into two equal groups of five. The notion of equal groups first appears when children learn the addition facts known as doubles, that is, 1 + 1, 2 + 2, 3 + 3, 4 + 4, 5 + 5, and so on.

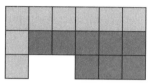

The number sentence that the children would be asked to write for the shape shown above would be 8 + 8 = 16, which comes from this family of doubles facts. These doubles form the basis for the first multiplication facts that children learn—multiplying by two. So, this simple task of covering a shape with tiles of two colors links addition, multiplication, division, and fractions.

Children may realize that the shapes that could be covered equally by two colors contain an even number of squares. Those that could not be covered in this way have an odd number of squares. The concept of odd and even numbers can be a difficult one for some children to grasp, and this visual representation of halves may make this concept understandable. With repeated visitations, children begin to discover that even numbers are those that can be divided into two equal-sized groups, and odd numbers are those that cannot. This approach, whereby children construct their own understanding, stands in sharp contrast to the traditional way, in which children are told that even numbers end in 2, 4, 6, 8, and 0 and odd numbers end in 1, 3, 5, 7, and 9.

Children use different strategies for checking their work. Some may guess and check by putting down some tiles of one color and then filling in the remaining squares with the other color and counting to see if an equal number of each color was used. Others may take turns placing a red tile, then a yellow, then a red, and so forth until the shape is covered. They may be aware that if each partner had an equal number of turns, then the shape must have been covered equally by each color. Other children may alternate tile colors until they fill up the shape, then count how many of each tile were placed on the shape. Still others may alternate placing tiles and then compare the number of unused tiles in each of their piles. If the number of unused tiles is equal, the shape was covered "half and half."

Some children may think that a color does not represent one half unless tiles of the same color are touching. For example, children who think this way would say that the rectangle on the left shows one half but that the rectangle on the right does not.

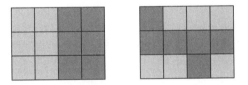

The ease with which Color Tiles may be rearranged makes it easy for a child to move the tiles in the rectangle on the right and reconfigure them to look like the rectangle on the left. Although the configuration of the tiles in each rectangle is different, the number sentences for the rectangles are identical: $6 + 6 = 12$. Combining these ideas may help broaden a child's understanding of the concept of one half.

As children find different ways to show halves, they have the opportunity to learn, demonstrate, and apply some of the basic concepts of fractions: that a fraction is composed of a number of parts that are equal in size and that the fraction used to name a part of a shape does not depend upon the absolute size of the shape.

HOW MANY RECTANGLES?

- Shape recognition
- Spatial visualization
- Comparing
- Properties of geometric shapes
- Congruence

Getting Ready

What You'll Need

Color Tiles, about 50 per pair

Color Tile grid paper, page 102

Construction paper

Glue

Overhead Color Tiles and/or Color Tile grid paper transparency (optional)

Overview

Children try to make as many different kinds of rectangles as possible using up to six Color Tiles. In this activity, children have the opportunity to:

- ◆ use spatial visualization to build shapes
- ◆ understand the characteristics of rectangles
- ◆ realize that orientation does not affect a rectangle's size or shape

The Activity

Introducing

- ◆ Ask children to tell what they know about rectangles.
- ◆ Draw a rectangle on the chalkboard.
- ◆ Then draw a square.
- ◆ Establish that rectangles can be different sizes and shapes and that a square is a special kind of rectangle.

On Their Own

> **How many different rectangles can you make using up to 6 Color Tiles?**
>
> - Work with a partner. Make as many different Color Tile rectangles as you can. You may use from 1 to 6 tiles for each rectangle.
> - Together, look over your rectangles. Make sure they are all different.
> - Record and cut out each different rectangle.
> - Glue each rectangle onto construction paper.
> - Count all your rectangles. Record that number.
> - Compare your rectangles. Be ready to talk about them.

The Bigger Picture

Thinking and Sharing

Invite one pair to post one of their rectangles and describe it while other children check to see if they have the same solution. Ask another pair to display a different solution. Continue until no one has a solution that is different from those on display.

Use prompts such as these to promote class discussion:

- How many different rectangles did you find?
- How did you find new rectangles?
- Were you sure that all your shapes were different from one another? How did you know?
- How can you be sure you found all the rectangles?
- What is the same about all the posted rectangles? What is different?
- How wide is that rectangle? (Point to one.) How long is it?
- What are some other things you notice when you look at the posted rectangles?

Writing

Have children use words, numbers, and pictures to tell what they know about rectangles made with up to six Color Tiles.

Extending the Activity

Have children find all the rectangles they can make using from one to nine Color Tiles.

Where's the Mathematics?

Children approach this activity in different ways. Some work in a random fashion, taking from one to six tiles at a time and arranging them into rectangles. It is only when children begin to realize that they are duplicating their efforts, or when they are asked how they can be sure that they have found all the rectangles, that they may begin to think about organizing the data in some way that allows them to look for a pattern. Other children like to organize their work as they go so that the number of tiles progresses from one to six in an orderly way.

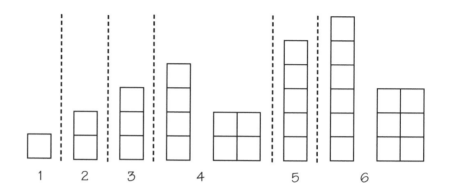

Another method by which some children may organize the rectangles is by one of their dimensions; that is, by putting all the rectangles that are one tile wide together and then all those that are two tiles wide together. Children are then likely to conclude that, using no more than six tiles altogether they cannot find any different rectangles three tiles wide (the 2 x 3 rectangle is already in the "2 tiles wide" column).

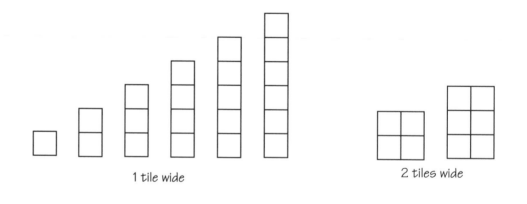

1 tile wide   2 tiles wide

Children who enjoy looking for number patterns may see some in the list of dimensions, noting that the first number remains 1 while the second number follows the sequence 1, 2, 3, 4, 5, 6, and then a similar pattern begins with 2 and then with 3, 4, 5, and 6. Listing dimensions in this way, however, gives six sets of duplicate rectangles: 1 x 2 and 2 x 1, 1 x 3 and 3 x 1, 2 x 3 and 3 x 2, 1 x 4 and 4 x 1, 1 x 5 and 5 x 1, 1 x 6 and 6 x 1.

1 x 1	2 x 1	3 x 1	4 x 1	5 x 1	6 x 1
1 x 2	2 x 2	3 x 2			
1 x 3	2 x 3				
1 x 4					
1 x 5					
1 x 6					

Some children may first perceive a shift in the orientation of a rectangle as a new shape. By putting one Color Tile rectangle over another, or by cutting the rectangles out of graph paper, children can manipulate their shapes to discover that what they thought were different shapes are really the same, or congruent, shapes. A child who understands this idea might look at the two rectangles below and say that the one on the right is just facing a different way.

Children have the opportunity to see that certain numbers can have more than one rectangular configuration. Naming the dimensions of each rectangle is akin to naming the factors each number has. For example, four tiles may be arranged as a 1 x 4 rectangle or a 2 x 2 square, and the factors of four are one, two, and four. For older children who are almost ready to begin multiplication, this activity makes a nice connection between geometry and number.

IT'S A FRAME-UP!

- Counting
- Creating patterns
- Comparing

Getting Ready

What You'll Need

Color Tiles, 40-50 per child

It's a Frame-Up! worksheet, page 95

Crayons

Overhead Color Tiles and/or Color Tile grid paper transparency (optional)

Overview

Children use Color Tiles to create a frame design that has a repeating color pattern. In this activity, children have an opportunity to:

- ◆ work with patterns that form a continuous loop
- ◆ compare patterns for similarities and differences

The Activity

Introducing

- ◆ Start to form a circle of tiles using a red-yellow pattern. As you do so, have children describe the pattern and identify the part that is repeating.

- ◆ When you are nearly finished making the circle, discuss how you may have to make it a little bigger or smaller so that the pattern will be continuous without ending up with two reds or two yellows together.

- ◆ Now begin another circle with the pattern red-yellow-yellow-red-yellow-yellow. Again, ask a volunteer to describe the pattern and identify the part that is repeating.

- ◆ Call on another child to complete the circle. He or she should watch to see that the pattern is continuous all the way around.

- ◆ Follow the same procedure using a three- or four-color pattern.

On Their Own

> **Can you make a picture-frame design using a 2-, 3-, or 4-color pattern?**
>
> - Work on your own. Place Color Tiles on an outline that looks like the one shown here to make a pattern that repeats all around the frame.
>
>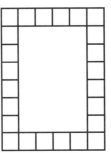
>
>   - If the pattern has 2 tiles, the 2 tiles must keep repeating.
>
>   - If the pattern has 3 tiles, the 3 tiles must keep repeating.
>
>   - If the pattern has 4 tiles, the 4 tiles must keep repeating.
>
> - Experiment until you make a design you like.
>
> - Record your picture-frame design by coloring the squares to match the tiles.

The Bigger Picture

Thinking and Sharing

Ask a volunteer to show and describe his or her picture-frame design. Post that design on the chalkboard. Call on children who think they have used the same pattern to hold up their work. If there is agreement, post each of these designs along with the first. Repeat this procedure with different patterns until all frame designs are on display.

Use prompts such as these to promote class discussion:

- How many repeats of the pattern does your frame have?

- How many tiles of each color did you need to complete your frame?

- How are these two frames alike? (Point to two frames.) How are they different?

- Were there any patterns you tried that didn't work when you got back to the starting point? If so, why didn't they work?

- How can the pattern on two frames be the same if their colors are not the same?

- Are there any patterns that many people made? that just one person made?

Extending the Activity

1. Give children a frame made up of thirty-six squares. Have them make designs for this frame based on patterns of two, three, or four tiles.

2. Have children design a frame within a frame; that is, a frame that is two tiles wide all the way around the picture.

Where's the Mathematics?

This activity presents a problem that artists and crafts people, such as quilt-makers, struggle with frequently: how to create a pattern that will continue smoothly around a perimeter. This is a far greater challenge than making a linear pattern; in order to be continuous, the repeat of the pattern must be a factor of the total number of tiles in the frame.

Because the frame used on the *It's a Frame-Up!* outline is made up of twenty-four squares, a pattern repeat must be either two, three, four, six, or twelve tiles long. Children will probably report that certain patterns, such as a five-tile *AABBB* pattern, did not work, because there were not enough uncovered squares left to finish the pattern when children got back to the starting point.

Even if children have chosen a pattern that will work, such as a four-tile *ABCD* pattern, they may still lose their place as they turn the corners and interrupt the continuity of the pattern. Notice what happened, for example, when a child who was creating an *ABCD* pattern turned the righthand corner, and started the pattern over by beginning with *A* instead of continuing the pattern by putting down *C*.

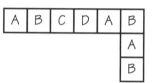

Children who experience this kind of problem may find it helpful to augment the visual pattern by reciting the colors involved; for example, "yellow-blue-red-green, yellow-blue-red-green," and so forth. By doing this, children are engaging their auditory sense so that it tunes into the rhythm that is involved in the pattern.

Many children are likely to use a two-tile *AB* pattern on their frame. Theoretically, using the four colors of the Color Tiles, children could make twelve different-colored *AB* patterns, as follows:

red-yellow	red-blue	red-green
green-yellow	green-blue	green-red
blue-yellow	blue-green	blue-red
yellow-red	yellow-blue	yellow-green

Identifying the common element of these patterns as alternating colors and calling it an *AB* pattern helps children to develop the ability to generalize. Being able to look at a multitude of data, locate the pattern, and generalize is an important skill in learning, especially in science and mathematics.

Questions about the number of repetitions and how many tiles of each color children need for their frames call forth a variety of solution strategies. Some children will simply count the individual tiles, whereas others may skip count. A few children may multiply the number of repetitions of their pattern by the number of tiles of each color needed for one repeat of the pattern. Some children may even recognize that they can count halfway around the frame and then double that number. Comparing the numbers that they have found will help children to see that frames with identical patterns have identical numbers of tiles. For example, if one child has a blue-yellow-yellow *ABB* pattern and another child has a red-green-green *ABB* pattern, both children have eight repeats of their pattern and need eight tiles of the *A* color and sixteen tiles of the *B* color to complete their frames.

LAST SURVIVOR

Getting Ready

What You'll Need

Color Tiles, 13 per pair

Overhead Color Tiles and/or Color Tile grid paper transparency (optional)

Overview

In this game for two players, children take turns removing one or two Color Tiles from a group of thirteen tiles in an effort to be the player who takes the last tile. In this activity, children have the opportunity to:

◆ develop strategic thinking skills

◆ count and develop one-to-one correspondence

◆ use mental mathematics to add and subtract

The Activity

If necessary, reduce the number of Color Tiles to fit the needs and abilities of your children.

Introducing

◆ Tell children that they will be playing a game called *Last Survivor.*

◆ Distribute Color Tiles to each pair of children and explain the game rules given in *On Their Own.*

◆ Demonstrate by playing a partial game of *Last Survivor,* either by yourself or with a volunteer.

On Their Own

Play _Last Survivor!_

Here are the rules.

1. This game is for 2 players. The object is to be the player who takes the last tile.

2. Players lay out 13 Color Tiles.

3. Players take turns removing 1 or 2 tiles at a time. No player may skip a turn.

4. The player who takes the last tile is the _Last Survivor_ and wins the game.

- Play several games of _Last Survivor_.

- Be ready to talk about good moves and bad moves.

The Bigger Picture

Thinking and Sharing

Invite children to talk about their games and describe some of the thinking they did.

Use prompts such as these to promote class discussion:

- How did you decide what moves to make?

- Did you find any strategies that worked? Explain.

- Does it matter who goes first? Explain.

- Is there a way to win every time?

- What would happen if you changed the number of tiles you started with?

Drawing and Writing

Have children use pictures and words to show a strategy for winning _Last Survivor_.

Extending the Activity

1. Repeat the activity but change the number of tiles children start with.

2. Repeat the activity but change the number of tiles children may take in a turn.

3. Have children play the game again, only this time the person left with the last tile loses the game.

Where's the Mathematics?

This game helps children develop, analyze, and compare strategies designed to produce a given outcome in a game situation. Most children at first play the game without any strategy in mind. Some will continue this way for a very long time. Other children may, after a while, begin to test a variety of strategies. A child may attempt a relatively random strategy, explaining, for example, that to win, "You should play any number until there are less than five left and then play very carefully."

Children sometimes test strategies that sound systematic but that are not based on an analysis of the situation. Copying what the other player does or thinking that the first person to play will always be the winner or the loser are examples of this. Children may develop a strategy, apply it successfully once, and be convinced that it will always work. With enough experience of playing this and other strategy games, children come to see that one success is not always enough to judge the validity of a strategy.

The key to winning in the game *Last Survivor* is for a player to control the number of tiles left on the table. The player with the advantage is the one who removes tiles so that a multiple of three (three, six, nine, or twelve) tiles is left on the table. Here is a scenario of how Player A, the player who goes first, can take control of the game and win by keeping track of sums of 3.

Player A takes one tile, leaving 12 (a multiple of 3) on the table. Then:

If player B takes	Player A takes	Sum of moves	Tiles left
1	2	1 + 2 = 3	9
2	1	2 + 1 = 3	6
2	1	2 + 1 = 3	3
1	2	1 + 2 = 3	0

If Player A goes second, he or she has to look for the earliest opportunity to leave either nine, six, or three tiles on the table. If Player B begins by taking two tiles, leaving eleven, Player A removes two and is in control again because nine tiles remain. If Player B begins the game by removing one, leaving twelve, there is no way Player A can get to nine tiles, so he or she has to wait. Taking just one tile leaves an opportunity for Player B to take just one also. If this happens, then Player A can regain control by taking one tile, leaving nine on the table. If this does not happen, Player A has to be patient and hope to regain control by the time he or she reaches six tiles. If both players know the strategy, the first player always wins.

As children describe their strategies, they should also try to explain how they arrived at them. Some children may have difficulty articulating what they are thinking. What is most important is to slowly develop the ability to reason out a situation and think ahead to predict the consequences of a particular action. If some children cannot come up with a winning strategy, it can be useful for them to listen to what others say and then try to implement the strategy they heard.

LINE UP FOUR

- **Counting**
- **Spatial visualization**
- **Deductive reasoning**
- **Game strategies**

Getting Ready

What You'll Need

Color Tiles, 8 of each of 2 colors

Line-Up Four game board, 1 per pair, page 96

Overhead Color Tiles and/or Color Tile grid paper transparency (optional)

Overview

In this game for two players, children take turns placing Color Tiles on the squares of a grid in an effort to be the first to line up four in a row. In this activity, children have the opportunity to:

- ◆ develop spatial reasoning
- ◆ develop strategic thinking skills

The Activity

Introducing

- ◆ Ask children if they know how to play *Tic-Tac-Toe*. Tell them that the game *Line Up Four* is something like it because in both games, each player tries to line up his or her pieces in a row.
- ◆ Go over the game rules given in *On Their Own*.
- ◆ Ask a volunteer to demonstrate the game with you.
- ◆ Play the game until someone lines up four tiles in a row, or until it is clear that no one can win.

On Their Own

Play *Line Up Four!*

Here are the rules:

1. This is a game for 2 players. The object is to be the first one to line up 4 tiles in a row in any direction on a game board.

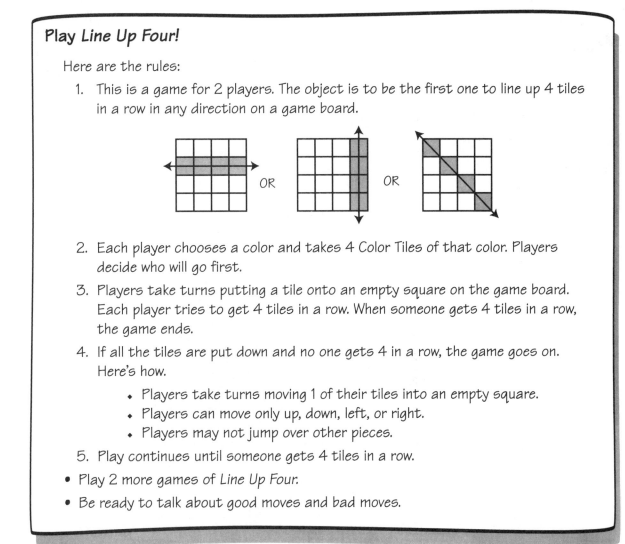

2. Each player chooses a color and takes 4 Color Tiles of that color. Players decide who will go first.

3. Players take turns putting a tile onto an empty square on the game board. Each player tries to get 4 tiles in a row. When someone gets 4 tiles in a row, the game ends.

4. If all the tiles are put down and no one gets 4 in a row, the game goes on. Here's how.

   • Players take turns moving 1 of their tiles into an empty square.
   • Players can move only up, down, left, or right.
   • Players may not jump over other pieces.

5. Play continues until someone gets 4 tiles in a row.

• Play 2 more games of *Line Up Four*.

• Be ready to talk about good moves and bad moves.

The Bigger Picture

Thinking and Sharing

Invite children to talk about their games and describe some of the thinking they did.

Use prompts like these to promote class discussion:

♦ Why is it important to pay attention to the other player's moves?

♦ What can you do to keep the other player from lining up four tiles in a row?

♦ Does anyone have a favorite first move? If so, describe that move. Why is it a good way to start?

♦ If you start by placing your tile in a corner, how many ways are there to line up four tiles in a row? What are they?

♦ Pick one of the inside squares. If you placed a tile on that square, how many ways could you get four tiles in a row? Explain.

♦ Are there any squares on the grid that you tried not to use? If so, which squares? Why didn't you want to use them?

Children may find it helpful to watch volunteers demonstrate playing strategies on a grid (or on an overhead grid).

Extending the Activity

1. Have children play the game again. This time if no one gets four in a row, allow them to continue playing by moving up, down, left, right, or diagonally.

Where's the Mathematics?

As they look for winning strategies and test those strategies, children develop logical thinking skills. They also gain some intuitive sense of probability as they consider all the possibilities for lining up four tiles in a row with each placement of their tiles.

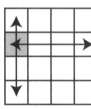 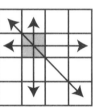 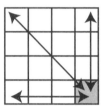

The center squares and the corners (numbered 1-8 below) provide the greatest number of opportunities to win, since lining up four tiles in a row may be accomplished vertically, horizontally, or diagonally using these spaces.

1			2
	3	4	
	5	6	
7			8

Children will probably indicate one of these eight squares as their favorite first move. The unnumbered spaces located along the edges provide only two opportunities to win: either vertically or horizontally. Children will probably report that they initially avoid using these spaces.

---

2. Have children play the game again. This time, if no one gets four in a row, allow them to continue playing by moving in any direction and by jumping over any one of the other player's tiles.

If no one wins *Line Up Four* after all eight of the Color Tiles are placed on the grid, then children are challenged to follow the rules for continuing the game by moving their tiles into a winning position. Finding a winning strategy, like being a good problem solver, requires perseverance and reflection. Thus, this game helps children develop ideas about problem solving. One such idea is that there is more than one way to win the game and, consequently, more than one way to solve a problem.

Playing the game several times in a row allows children an opportunity to refine their strategy and get immediate feedback on whether the new strategy is indeed an improvement. As children become aware that some moves are better than others, they learn that planning ahead can be very helpful in a game of strategy.

In this game, children must also pay attention to their opponent's play, blocking his or her moves as necessary. This encourages children to look at a problem from more than one point of view. Children must simultaneously plan ahead for their own moves while watching their opponent's moves and making adjustments in play based on what they see. If they play this game in teams, they gain additional insight into problem solving by seeing and hearing how other children approach the game.

Class discussions regarding the games will help children consciously reflect on their strategies. Many children in this age group will not be aware of how much thinking and strategizing they did until called upon to put the process into words. They are apt to think that winning was a matter of luck and not realize that a fair amount of skill was involved. Armed with some good strategies for winning, this may prove to be a popular game for children to take home and share with their families.

MIRROR, MIRROR ON THE WALL

- Symmetry
- Spatial visualization

Getting Ready

What You'll Need

Color Tiles, about 30 per group

Paper, 12" x 18", 1 sheet per group

Rulers

Overhead Color Tiles and/or Color Tile grid paper transparency (optional)

Overview

Children create Color Tile shapes that have horizontal or vertical line symmetry. In this activity, children have the opportunity to:

- ◆ complete a symmetrical shape, piece by piece
- ◆ discuss whether or not a design has symmetry

The Activity

Working in threes during the On Their Own *activity ensures that children take turns placing new tiles and balancing the symmetry of the design.*

Introducing

- ◆ Draw a thick vertical line down the center of a sheet of paper and display it. Place a Color Tile so that one of its edges lies along this vertical line.

- ◆ Invite a volunteer to place a Color Tile of the same color on the paper to make a shape that is symmetrical. Explain that the tile must be on the other side of the line so that when you trace the tiles and fold the paper along the line, the two sides will cover each other exactly.

- ◆ Trace around the two tiles, fold the paper along the line, and verify that the shape is symmetrical.

- ◆ Unfold the paper and put the two tiles back as they were. Then invite two volunteers to come up, one at a time. Have the first child place a tile on one side of the line of symmetry so that it is touching at least one of the tiles already placed there. Have the next child place a tile of the same color on the other side so that it looks like a reflection of the tile just put down, thus keeping the shape symmetrical.

- ◆ Repeat this process with other volunteers.

On Their Own

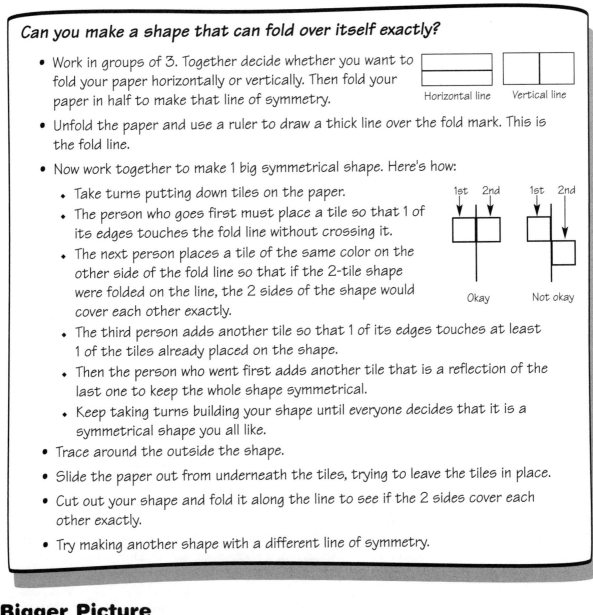

Can you make a shape that can fold over itself exactly?

- Work in groups of 3. Together decide whether you want to fold your paper horizontally or vertically. Then fold your paper in half to make that line of symmetry.

Horizontal line   Vertical line

- Unfold the paper and use a ruler to draw a thick line over the fold mark. This is the fold line.

- Now work together to make 1 big symmetrical shape. Here's how:

  - Take turns putting down tiles on the paper.
  - The person who goes first must place a tile so that 1 of its edges touches the fold line without crossing it.
  - The next person places a tile of the same color on the other side of the fold line so that if the 2-tile shape were folded on the line, the 2 sides of the shape would cover each other exactly.

1st 2nd   1st 2nd

Okay   Not okay

  - The third person adds another tile so that 1 of its edges touches at least 1 of the tiles already placed on the shape.
  - Then the person who went first adds another tile that is a reflection of the last one to keep the whole shape symmetrical.
  - Keep taking turns building your shape until everyone decides that it is a symmetrical shape you all like.

- Trace around the outside the shape.

- Slide the paper out from underneath the tiles, trying to leave the tiles in place.

- Cut out your shape and fold it along the line to see if the 2 sides cover each other exactly.

- Try making another shape with a different line of symmetry.

The Bigger Picture

Thinking and Sharing

Have each group select its favorite symmetrical shape and help children to post these shapes. Invite each group to explain how they went about making their posted shape.

Use prompts such as these to promote class discussion:

- Which was easier to work with, the horizontal or vertical fold line? Why?
- Were some tiles harder to place than others? Explain.
- Which job did you like better, placing a tile or making the shape symmetrical? Why?
- How does folding help to show that the two parts of a shape are exactly the same?
- Did you have any other way of knowing if the parts matched? If so, tell how.
- Does your shape have another fold line, or line of symmetry? How can you tell?
- Where are the lines of symmetry on a single Color Tile?

Extending the Activity

1. Have children use glue and construction-paper squares to recreate their designs on paper.

2. After children have completed placing all the tiles in their symmetrical design, have them take turns removing any tile from one side of the

Teacher Talk

Where's the Mathematics?

This activity gives children a chance to use reflective, or line, symmetry creatively in a setting where they take turns working with other children. By building their symmetrical shapes one tile at a time, children become deeply involved in noticing how each component contributes to the symmetrical outcome of the shape. Children are likely to report that the vertical line of symmetry was slightly easier to work with than the horizontal line. This may be due to the fact that objects with a vertical line of symmetry—for example, people, buildings, and trees—are more abundant in the environment than are those with horizontal lines of symmetry. Thus, children are already familiar with vertical lines of symmetry on an intuitive level. (Where children sit in relation to the line of symmetry may, of course, turn a horizontal line into a vertical line, and vice versa.)

This activity is deceptively easy at the start, but becomes more complicated as the shape grows. The colors of the tiles help many children to stay oriented and to know where to place the next tile. As the shape grows, many children rely on counting to ensure that they place the tiles properly. They may reason, "The green tile is one, two, three tiles over on this side, so I will put another green tile three tiles over on the other side." The balance of a symmetrical shape also helps many children intuitively know where to place the next tile in order to maintain that balance.

Some children simply create a mosaic pattern, whereas others like to have a real object in mind. For example, the following shape might be seen as the reflection of a building on a lake.

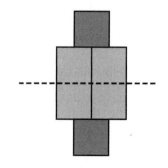

design and then removing its reflected tile from the other side of the design. Children should keep taking turns removing tiles until no more tiles remain.

3. Repeat the activity but change the rules so that, on each turn, children place two tiles on the paper.

Since a Color Tile is a square, it has four lines of symmetry:

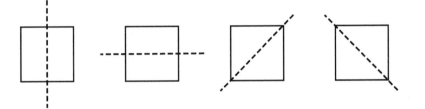

Some children already know this and others may discover it while building their symmetrical shapes. Because tiles have multiple lines of symmetry, some children's work, too, may have more than one line of symmetry, especially early on in the process of building the shape. As the shapes become more complicated, these multiple lines of symmetry may disappear.

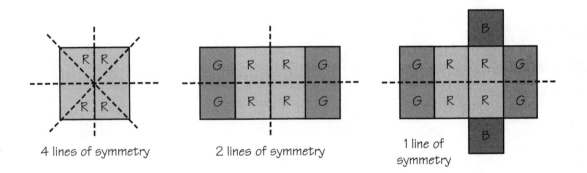

4 lines of symmetry   2 lines of symmetry   1 line of symmetry

---

MIRROR, MIRROR ON THE WALL ◆ Color Tiles ◆ Grades K-2   **69**

MYSTERY PATTERNS

Getting Ready

What You'll Need

Color Tiles, about 20-24 per pair

Mystery Patterns Clue Cards,
1 set per pair, pages 97-98

Mystery Patterns Color Tile Strips,
page 99

Crayons

Overhead Color Tiles and/or Color
Tile grid paper transparency (optional)

Overview

Children use clues to make patterns with Color Tiles. In this activity, children have the opportunity to:

- work with patterns
- reason deductively

The Activity

Explain that A means that the first tile is one color and B means that the second tile is a different color. An ABA pattern would mean that the first and third tiles are the same color and the second tile is a different color.

In preparation for On Their Own, copy and cut apart the clue cards for each pair.

Introducing

- Display the repetition of an *AB* pattern using yellow and blue Color Tiles.

- Ask children to describe the pattern and identify the part that is repeated.

- Tell children you can describe the pattern by giving this clue: *It is an AB pattern.* Write this clue on the chalkboard.

- Ask volunteers for additional clues that describe the pattern and write these on the chalkboard also. Four clues for your pattern might be:

  > It is an AB *pattern.*
  > The second tile is blue.
  > There is no red or green.
  > Yellow is A.

- Have children read the clues. Establish that they can make a Color Tile pattern without seeing it first, as long as they have good clues that describe it.

On Their Own

Can you build the Color Tile mystery patterns described on the clue cards?

- Work with a partner. Choose a clue card and read the clues aloud.

- Use the clues to try to build the mystery pattern with your Color Tiles.

- When you both think you have built the mystery pattern, read the clues again. Then check your work. Make changes if you need to.

- Record your pattern by coloring squares on a Color Tile strip. Write the number of the mystery pattern on the back of the strip.

- Select another clue card and repeat the activity.

- Be ready to talk about how you built the mystery patterns.

The Bigger Picture

Thinking and Sharing

Write the clue card numbers,*#1, #2,* and so on across the chalkboard. Have pairs of children post solutions under the appropriate headings.

Use prompts like these to promote class discussion:

- Which mystery patterns were easy to build? Which were hard? Why?

- How did you go about building a mystery pattern?

- Did you change the pattern as you worked? Why or why not?

- (Read one clue aloud—for example, "B is not green".) What can you learn from this clue? What do you still need to find out?

- Are all the posted patterns the same? If not, explain.

- Why was it important to read the clues again after you had built the mystery pattern?

Writing

Have children create their own Color Tile mystery patterns by starting with a simple pattern and then writing four clues that describe it. Groups can trade clues and try to solve one another's mystery patterns.

Extending the Activity

1. Repeat the activity, but give children more complex patterns and clues.

2. Have children solve mystery patterns that you have created for other manipulatives such as Pattern Blocks, Cuisenaire® Rods, Tangrams, or Snap™ Cubes.

Where's the Mathematics?

Pattern recognition is the focus of much of the work children do in the primary grades. This activity provides an interesting twist by presenting clues challenging children to use them to build a pattern that fits the clues. Thus, the activity provides a bridge that connects patterns with logical thinking, whereby children analyze clues and eliminate certain possibilities.

Some children will draw a conclusion based on just one clue. These children will begin to learn that they must read the entire clue card before jumping to such conclusions, because there is not enough information in one clue to narrow down all the possible patterns. For example, consider the clue "It is an *ABB* pattern" which leads to the conclusion that the pattern consists of three tiles and has two colors, one color in the first position and the other in both the second and third positions. However, this clue tells nothing about which colors are involved, and so there are twelve possibilities.

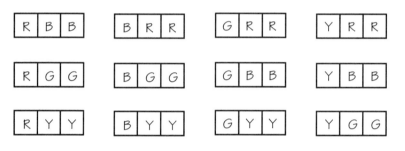

If the next clue stated "*B* is not green," children can conclude that *B* must be either red or yellow or blue. Combining this clue with the first clue eliminates three of the above possibilities and leaves these nine.

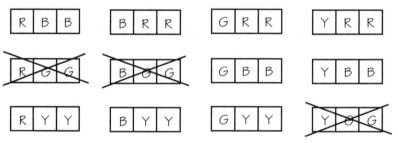

The remaining clues should continue to remove possibilities from consideration and bring children to the mystery pattern or patterns.

Most children will not work in terms of all the possibilities for each clue but will probably come up with a single candidate pattern based on the information gained with each successive clue. Here is an example of how this method might play out with pattern #4:

Clue	Candidate Pattern
1. It has 3 colors.	yellow-red-green
2. There is no red.	yellow-blue-green
3. The name of the last color begins with a Y.	blue-green-yellow
4. The middle color is not green.	green-blue-yellow

Children generally have more difficulty with the clues that include the *not* or *no*, such as "The first tile is not yellow" or "There is no red." These negative clues, rather than give an exact location for a color in a pattern, eliminate a possibility. It may benefit children during the class discussion to practice translating such negative clues into positive ones: "The first tile is red, green, or blue," or "The tiles in the pattern may be green, blue, or yellow."

Some children forget things not specifically mentioned in the clues. For example, the clues for the first pattern mention that the *ABC* pattern does not have green and that yellow comes first and red comes last. A key piece of information, namely that the pattern does not contain blue, is missing. Children have to "read between the lines" and not forget that any of the four colors is an option.

Children frequently forget to go back and combine new information with what they already know. Looking back over the work is an important part of good problem solving, particularly when logic is involved. In making patterns from clues, children should observe that one faulty conclusion can lead to a series of errors in later logic. Hearing the clues again and looking at their work critically can help children identify errors and open up the possibility of additional solutions.

Older children might enjoy writing clue cards for mystery patterns as much as solving the mysteries. Thinking about the amount of information needed to create a pattern that is solvable and then writing the clues down can take some of the anxiety out of dealing with word problems that children encounter throughout their study of mathematics.

SQUARE BY SQUARE

Getting Ready

What You'll Need

Color Tiles, 70 per pair

Square-by-Square game board, 1 per child, page 100

Number cubes with faces numbered 1, 2, and 3, 2 per pair

Overhead Color Tiles and/or Color Tile grid paper transparency (optional)

Overview

In this game for two players, children take turns rolling number cubes and finding the sum of the numbers rolled to determine the number of Color Tiles to put on a game board. In this activity, children have the opportunity to:

◆ use one, two, and three as addends

◆ use spatial reasoning

◆ develop strategic thinking skills

The Activity

Prepare the number cubes needed for the game by marking the numbers 1, 2, and 3 on opposite faces of color cubes.

Introducing

◆ Tell children that they will be playing a game called *Square by Square*.

◆ Present the game rules given in *On Their Own*. Be sure that children understand that *vertical* describes a line that goes up and down, and *horizontal* describes a line that goes from side to side.

◆ Demonstrate how to play *Square by Square* by playing a partial game, either by yourself or with a partner.

On Their Own

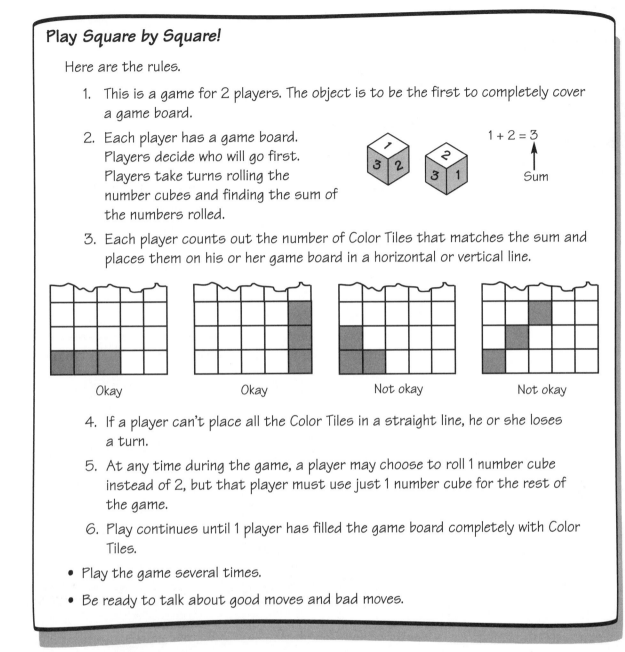

Play *Square by Square!*

Here are the rules.

1. This is a game for 2 players. The object is to be the first to completely cover a game board.

2. Each player has a game board. Players decide who will go first. Players take turns rolling the number cubes and finding the sum of the numbers rolled.

   $1 + 2 = 3$

   Sum

3. Each player counts out the number of Color Tiles that matches the sum and places them on his or her game board in a horizontal or vertical line.

   Okay   Okay   Not okay   Not okay

4. If a player can't place all the Color Tiles in a straight line, he or she loses a turn.

5. At any time during the game, a player may choose to roll 1 number cube instead of 2, but that player must use just 1 number cube for the rest of the game.

6. Play continues until 1 player has filled the game board completely with Color Tiles.

- Play the game several times.
- Be ready to talk about good moves and bad moves.

The Bigger Picture

Thinking and Sharing

Invite children to talk about their games and describe some of the thinking they did.

Use prompts such as these to promote class discussion:

- What tips would you suggest to help someone win?
- Did you lose a turn very often? If so, why do you think that happened?
- Why do you think the game rules let you use one number cube? When would you tell a player to use one number cube?

Extending the Activity

1. Change the size of the game board and the numbers on one or both of the number cubes to adapt the game for children with higher level skills.

2. Modify the game to use multiplication. Children put Color Tiles on the game board that form a rectangle as wide as the number on the one

Teacher Talk

Where's the Mathematics?

This activity is a strategy game with embedded addition practice. For children who are still developing their addition skills, the use of Color Tiles provides a concrete representation of the addition process. Rolling the number cubes adds an element of chance so that children with weak addition skills are not at a disadvantage when playing against children with better skills.

It will not take children long to learn that the game board is only five squares wide. If children focus solely on covering these rows of five, they will be frustrated due to the limited ways in which this can be done. Since the only possible sums are 2 (1 + 1), 3 (1 + 2), 4 (1 + 3, or 2 + 2), 5 (2 + 3), and 6 (3 + 3), the only way to fill the row is to roll a sum of 5 or to roll a sum of 2 and a sum of 3; a roll of 6 results in a lost turn.

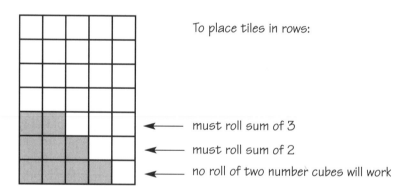

To place tiles in rows:

← must roll sum of 3

← must roll sum of 2

← no roll of two number cubes will work

On the other hand, if children focus on filling the game board in vertical columns, they have seven squares to work with and space for larger sums, such as 3 + 3 and 3 + 2.

number cube and as tall as the number on the other cube. For example, if a 2 and 3 were rolled, the player would use Color Tiles to form a 2 x 3 rectangle and place it on the board. Since players would need to roll two 1s to cover one square 1 tile wide by 1 tile high, they would use two number cubes all the way to the end.

With experience, children come to realize that they should avoid creating small pockets of uncovered spaces. In the game shown on the following game board, suppose that a 1 + 1 has just been rolled.

If the child using this game board places the tiles on the spaces numbered *2* and *3*, a single uncovered space will be left in the upper lefthand corner. A better move would be to place the tiles on spaces *1* and *2*. An even better move would be to cover spaces *4* and *5*. Through trial and error, children learn such strategies. Children also gradually see the advantage of filling in small areas and leaving larger spaces open as the game progresses. You may find that children are very savvy about placing their tiles even though they may not be able to articulate why they placed the tiles as they did.

Children quickly learn that they should wait to use one number cube until most, if not all, of the uncovered spaces on their game board form lines of three or fewer squares. Using the option prematurely means that the rest of a child's game board will be covered more slowly, leaving the way open for an opponent who is still rolling two number cubes to win.

The numbers on one or both of the number cubes can be easily changed to adapt the skill level to match that of the children who are playing the game. In a multilevel class, everyone can be playing the same game but at different levels. The size of the game board can, of course, also be changed to match the relative size of the numbers on the number cubes.

VERY BUSY ANIMALS

- **Counting**
- **Estimation**
- **Computation**

Getting Ready

What You'll Need

Color Tiles, 55 per pair
Crayons

Overview

Children use Color Tiles to figure out the total number of animals in a nonsense rhyme in which addends keep increasing by one. In this activity, children have the opportunity to:

- ◆ estimate a sum
- ◆ count and calculate in context
- ◆ notice a predictable growth pattern

The Activity

With younger children, you may want to model working out the first couple of lines using Color Tiles. Ask such questions as "How many tiles should I take for the lion? How many for the dogs?"

You may also want to read about only five animals and ask children to figure out just that much. This offers children a problem that is challenging but not overwhelming.

Introducing

- ◆ Prepare a chart with the words to the rhyme *Very Busy Animals*, which are presented in *On Their Own*.
- ◆ Post the chart and invite the class to read along as you read the words aloud.
- ◆ Give children a chance to react to the rhyme.
- ◆ Ask children how many lions were flying and how many dogs sat on logs. Then ask how many animals altogether were busy flying or sitting on logs. Have children explain how they know this.

On Their Own

How many animals altogether are very busy doing different things?

- Work with a partner. Read this rhyme softly together.

1 lion flying	6 kangaroos tying their shoes
2 dogs sitting on logs	7 pigs eating figs
3 cats wearing hats	8 ants doing a dance
4 foxes hiding in boxes	9 seals walking on their heels
5 parrots nibbling on carrots	10 poodles serving noodles

- Make an estimate, or guess, about how many animals there are altogether. Record this number.

- Now use Color Tiles to help you to figure out the answer.

- Show how you solved the problem. Use words, numbers, and drawings.

The Bigger Picture

Thinking and Sharing

Invite pairs to talk about how they went about solving the problem.

Use prompts such as these to promote discussion:

- How did you make your estimate before you began to work with the tiles?

- Was the number of animals in your estimate greater or fewer than the real number?

- How did you use the tiles to solve the problem?

- How did you go about counting the tiles? Do you think counting them in groups is easier than counting them one at a time? Why?

- Did you notice how the number of animals increased as the rhyme went on? If so, tell how.

Extending the Activity

1. Have children repeat the activity, but this time change the rhyme using only even numbers. (2 dogs sitting on logs, 4 foxes hiding, and so on.)

2. Look for children's literature to provide other rich problem-solving scenarios that involve growing patterns. Some examples are *One Gorilla, Ten Black Dots,* and *Twelve Circus Rings.*

Where's the Mathematics?

In this activity, children work with a predictable growth pattern. With each new group of animals, the group size increases by one. A growth pattern of this sort, which increases or decreases by adding or subtracting a constant number at each step in a sum, is called an *arithmetic series*.

The pattern 1 + 2 + 3 +... appears in mathematical situations such as counting, staircase patterns, and triangular numbers. This pattern also occurs in many children's stories and poems. When young children work with this simple growth pattern, they reinforce their familiarity with counting. Using concrete objects to build the pattern helps children go beyond rote counting to develop their sense of quantity.

When asked to find the total number of animals, many children begin by counting out the number of Color Tiles that corresponds to each line of the rhyme. Children may then place the tiles in rows or columns, keeping each group of animals separate. After this, some children simply move in order from 1 to 10, adding the numbers on one at a time and finding an ever-growing sum.

Some children may need to write down each set of addends and its sum like this:

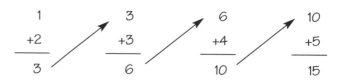

Other children may just write the sum from each addition problem and use the tiles as they count on. A few children may be able to find the sums and count on mentally all the way through the problem.

Children who are visual learners may count out the Color Tiles to represent each line of the rhyme and then move the tiles around on their desk, grouping them by twos, fives, or tens, using whichever grouping makes the most sense to them and is easiest for them to count with mentally.

If children have worked with forming groups of 10, they may notice how neatly this series lends itself to making such groups: The 1 can be placed on top of the 9, the 2 on top of the 8, the 3 on top of the 7, and the 4 on top of the 6, forming five columns of 10 plus 5 tiles left in the 5 column, for a grand total of 55.

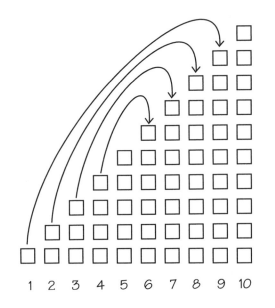

1 2 3 4 5 6 7 8 9 10

Children may also notice this same pattern if they write the numbers in the rhyme as a column of numbers to be added.

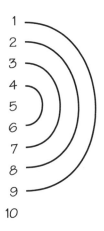

Grouping numbers together to facilitate addition is formally called the *associative property of addition*. Looking at how grouping the numbers in sets of ten makes the addition easier underscores for children the meaning of our base-ten number system.

Sharing different solution strategies for this problem can help children broaden their view of mathematics and make them more flexible in their approach to problem solving.

WHAT'S IN THE BAG?

- Counting
- Deductive reasoning

Getting Ready

What You'll Need

Color Tiles, 20 per pair

Small paper bags stapled shut, 2 per pair, one labeled "Riddle 1" and the other labeled "Riddle 2," and containing the following Color Tiles:

Riddle 1: 1 red, 2 yellow, 4 blue
Riddle 2: 3 red, 3 yellow, 2 green

Sample Riddle Bag containing 2 blue and 4 yellow tiles

Crayons

Overhead Color Tiles and/or Color Tile grid paper transparency (optional)

The Activity

You may prefer to make up your own clues, adjusting the level of difficulty to suit children in your particular class.

Overview

Children solve riddles to discover the number and colors of Color Tiles that are hidden in a paper bag. In this activity, children have the opportunity to:

- ◆ build logical reasoning skills
- ◆ explain how they reasoned logically
- ◆ count and relate numerical quantities

Introducing

- ◆ Hold up the sample Riddle Bag containing two blue and four yellow tiles. Explain that you will give some clues so that children can try to figure out the number and colors of Color Tiles in the bag.

- ◆ Tell children to use Color Tiles to keep track of the information they learn from your clues.

- ◆ Give the first clue: *I have six tiles in my bag.* Have children follow this clue by counting out six tiles.

- ◆ Have children respond to the second clue: *The tiles are of two different colors.*

- ◆ Give two more clues, pausing after each to allow children time to adjust their tiles to match it:
    There are no red or green tiles.
    There are four yellow tiles.

- ◆ Have children display their solutions to the riddle. Then reveal the contents of the Riddle Bag.

- ◆ Discuss what makes a good riddle clue. Help children to see that each new clue should bring the solution closer.

On Their Own

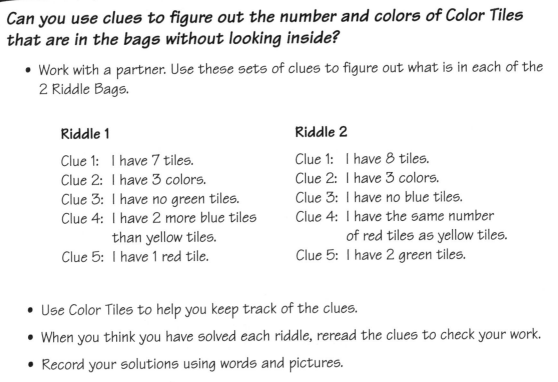

Can you use clues to figure out the number and colors of Color Tiles that are in the bags without looking inside?

- Work with a partner. Use these sets of clues to figure out what is in each of the 2 Riddle Bags.

Riddle 1

Clue 1: I have 7 tiles.
Clue 2: I have 3 colors.
Clue 3: I have no green tiles.
Clue 4: I have 2 more blue tiles than yellow tiles.
Clue 5: I have 1 red tile.

Riddle 2

Clue 1: I have 8 tiles.
Clue 2: I have 3 colors.
Clue 3: I have no blue tiles.
Clue 4: I have the same number of red tiles as yellow tiles.
Clue 5: I have 2 green tiles.

- Use Color Tiles to help you keep track of the clues.

- When you think you have solved each riddle, reread the clues to check your work.

- Record your solutions using words and pictures.

- Do not open the bags until later.

The Bigger Picture

Thinking and Sharing

Ask children to delay opening their riddle bags until they share their solutions and discuss the reasoning behind them.

Use prompts such as these to promote class discussion:

- How did you go about solving Riddle 1? Riddle 2?
- How did you figure out which colors are in each bag?
- How did you figure how many of each color are in each bag?
- Did you need all the clues for each riddle? Why or why not?
- Was one riddle easier to solve than the other? If so, why?
- Why was it important to reread the clues after you figured out the contents?

Extending the Activity

1. Have children create their own Riddle Bags by laying out seven to twelve Color Tiles and writing five clues about them. Then have children put the tiles in a bag, staple their riddle to the bag, and exchange them. Here is a structural model for children to follow: Clue 1: Number of tiles

Teacher Talk

Where's the Mathematics?

Logical thinking is closely tied to language development. By giving children many experiences both in listening to and using mathematical language, you give children an opportunity to increase their vocabulary and their understanding of mathematical concepts. This activity uses a riddle format to enhance logical thinking while building number concepts. It also prepares children to sift through words in order to find the key numbers and concepts necessary for solving word problems.

Children will use deductive reasoning to analyze clues, eliminate possibilities, and organize information. The riddles give children practice in combining isolated bits of information to make one complete whole. The clues in the first two riddles are not organized in the most straightforward manner. Children may point out that it is best to read an entire riddle first before trying to solve any of the clues. Doing this makes it possible to organize the clues from most useful to least useful and to attack the problem more efficiently. In Riddle 1, the fifth clue is probably the best place to start because it contains very specific information. Then, combining the second and third clues establishes that the bag contains only red, yellow, and blue tiles. Looking at the fourth clue will probably require the most analysis. Counting out one yellow tile and three blue tiles would satisfy this clue. One might think that combining those four tiles with the one red tile might work until one considers the first clue and realizes that a total of seven tiles is needed. Adjusting the blue and yellow tiles will finally yield a solution of one red, two yellow, and four blue tiles.

in the bag; Clue 2: Number of colors in the bag; Clue 3: Colors not in the bag; Clue 4: A comparison of the numbers of two colors of tiles; Clue 5: The number of one color of tiles.

2. Create Riddle Bags for children using another manipulative such as Pattern Blocks, Cuisenaire® Rods, Tangrams, or Connecting People.

Some children may think that all of the clues are vitally important. However, in both riddles, either the second or third clues could be eliminated without losing any critical information. Combining the fourth and fifth clues in each of the two riddles provides information about the colors in the bag so that only the second or third clue is needed to confirm that the bag does not contain a fourth color.

Children frequently forget to go back and combine the new information revealed by a clue with information contained in previous clues. Rereading the entire riddle will ensure that children have not overlooked important information given earlier in the riddle. Learning to look back is an important final step in problem solving; reminding children to practice this important problem-solving step will help train them to solve more complicated problems in the future.

Older children enjoy writing riddles as much as they enjoy solving them. Having the tiles on the table in front of them before they start writing their riddles and using the format suggested makes writing riddles almost easy! The fourth clue may present the greatest challenge, but learning how to phrase these clues will help children to understand the wording they will encounter in solving word problems.

WHO'S GOT THE BIGGEST YARD?

- Counting
- Estimation
- Area
- Comparing

Getting Ready

What You'll Need

Color Tiles, 20 per pair

Dog Yards outline, 1 per child, page 101

Overhead Color Tiles and/or Color Tile grid paper transparency (optional)

2" x 3" rectangle drawn on overhead transparency or sheet of paper

Overview

Children estimate and then find, the number of Color Tiles required to cover the areas of various shapes. Then they order the shapes according to area. In this activity, children have the opportunity to:

- find the area of different shapes
- compare different areas
- explore the relationship between shape and area
- develop estimation skills

The Activity

Introducing

- Display a drawing of a 2" x 3" rectangle. Ask children to estimate how many Color Tiles it will take to cover the rectangle.
- After several estimates have been given, place Color Tiles on the rectangle.
- Together with the class, count the number of Color Tiles covering the shape. Establish that there are six.
- Explain that the number of squares required to cover a figure is called its *area* and that the area of this rectangle is six Color Tiles.

On Their Own

Can you estimate and then measure to tell which of 3 rectangles will contain the most Color Tiles?

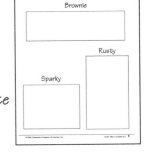

- Work with a partner. Look at the drawings of Brownie's, Sparky's, and Rusty's yards on a worksheet that look like this. Talk about how you think the sizes of the yards compare.

- Now look at the drawing of Brownie's yard. Estimate how many Color Tiles would cover it exactly. Record your estimate on the drawing.

- Place Color Tiles on the drawing to check your estimate. Record your results next to your estimate.

- Compare the 2 numbers you recorded.

- Next, look at the drawing of Sparky's yard. Estimate how many Color Tiles would cover it exactly. Record your estimate on the drawing.

- Place Color Tiles on the drawing to check your estimate. Record these results next to your estimate. Compare the 2 numbers.

- Repeat this process with the drawing of Rusty's yard.

- Now cut out the 3 drawings and arrange them in order from the smallest yard to the biggest yard.

- Be ready to talk about anything that surprised you.

The Bigger Picture

Thinking and Sharing

Invite children to share their responses to this activity.

Use prompts like these to promote class discussion:

- How many Color Tiles did you estimate it would take to cover _____'s yard? How many tiles did it actually take to cover that yard?

- How close were your estimates to the actual numbers?

- Did you use any shortcuts for finding the area after you measured the first yard? If so, share them.

- Can you predict how many tiles it will take to cover a yard just by looking at it? What makes this easy or hard?

- In what order would you arrange the dogs' yards, from smallest to biggest? Do you think you could have done this just by looking at the three drawings? Why or why not?

- How much larger is the biggest yard than the smallest yard? How did you figure that out?

Extending the Activity

1. Have children use Color Tiles to measure the area of a book cover. Then have them try to find a book of a different shape with an area that is about the same.

Where's the Mathematics?

Giving children concrete experiences with measuring area lays the groundwork for understanding that area is a measure of the amount of space that a shape covers. This prepares children to make sense of area formulas they will later be taught. Color Tiles are ideal for this kind of investigation because they help children to see how square units can be used to measure two-dimensional shapes.

Children should discover that Rusty has the biggest yard, Brownie has the next biggest, and Sparky the smallest.

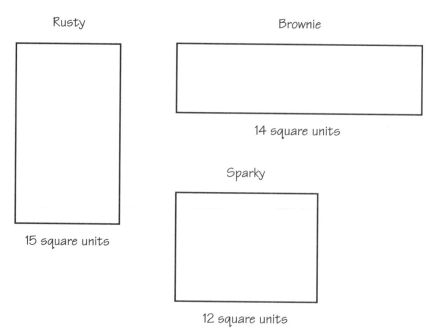

Rusty

Brownie

14 square units

15 square units

Sparky

12 square units

Being able to estimate the areas of different rectangles depends partly on a child's understanding of the size and shape of a Color Tile. The accuracy of many children's estimates may improve as they gain additional experience with the size of the Color Tiles relative to the size of the rectangles they are covering. Even so, predictions about the area of a rectangles can be tricky: Even when the areas of two rectangles are the same, the eye can be deceived into thinking that a long, thin rectangle has a greater area than a short, wide one.

2. Have children investigate how many different rectangles can be made using exactly twelve tiles.

Some children will devise shortcuts for finding the number of tiles that will cover a yard. For example, they might cover just one row of Brownie's yard with seven tiles, see that the yard is half covered, and then, without actually doing the covering, conclude that one more row of seven will complete the job. Similarly, they could use six tiles to cover two columns of Sparky's yard and recognize that six more tiles would be needed without placing them down.

Children may come up with a variety of ways for telling how much larger the biggest yard is than the smallest. Some may cover both yards with tiles and partition the tiles in the bigger yard so that one of the partitions matches the smaller yard. Then they can count the number of leftover tiles in the bigger yard to conclude that Rusty's yard is three Color Tiles bigger than Sparky's.

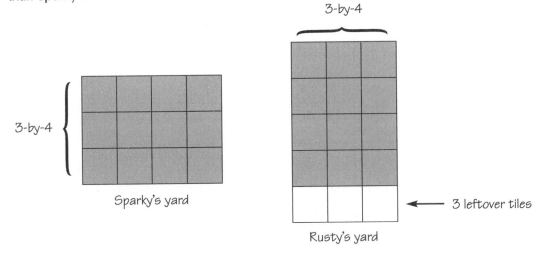

3-by-4

3-by-4

Sparky's yard

Rusty's yard

← 3 leftover tiles

Others may just look at the numbers they get for Sparky's and Rusty's yards and count up from 12 to 15. Still others—probably older children—will be able to subtract to find the answer.

Instead of estimating, some children may at first simply guess. Then, as they find the actual area of a shape, children may begin to form estimation strategies. For example, they may compare a shape with an unknown area to one whose area they have already found.

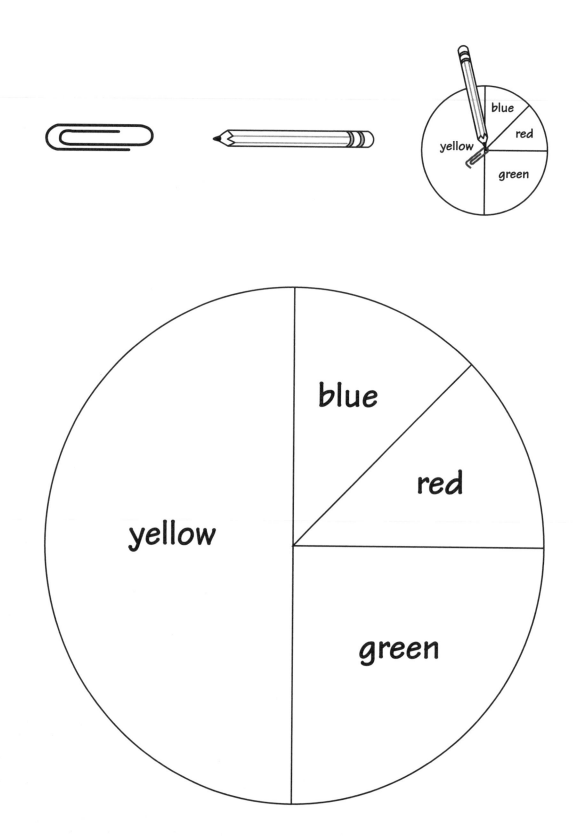

I named my creature _____.

I used _____ Color Tiles to make my creature.

I used _____ reds

_____ greens

_____ yellows

_____ blues

Here are other facts about my creature.

_____

_____

_____

_____

_____

_____

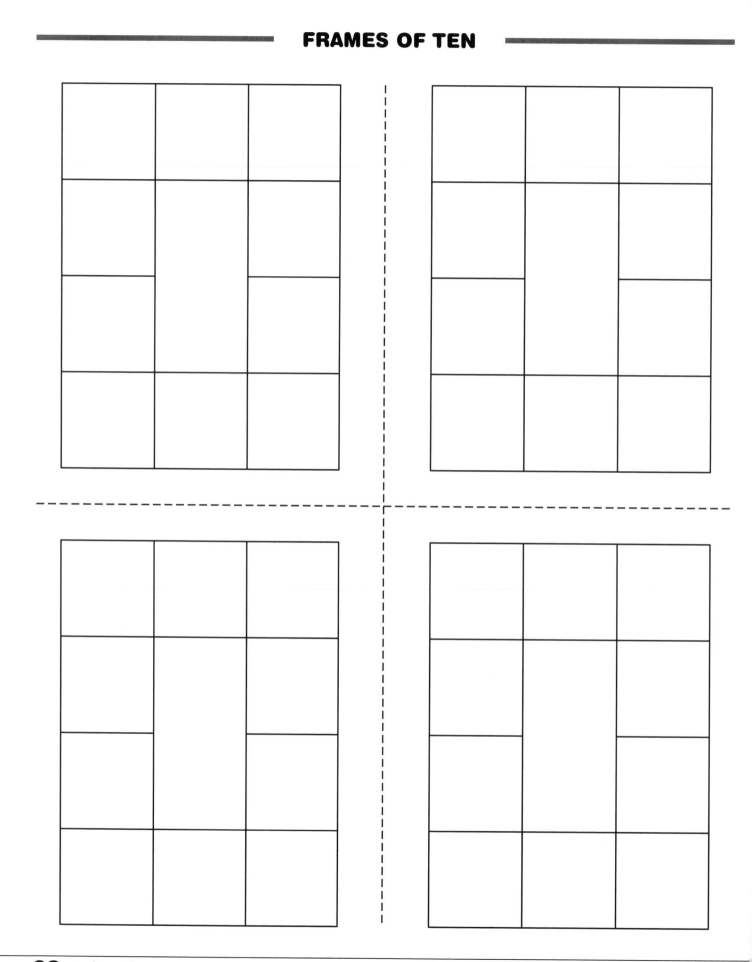

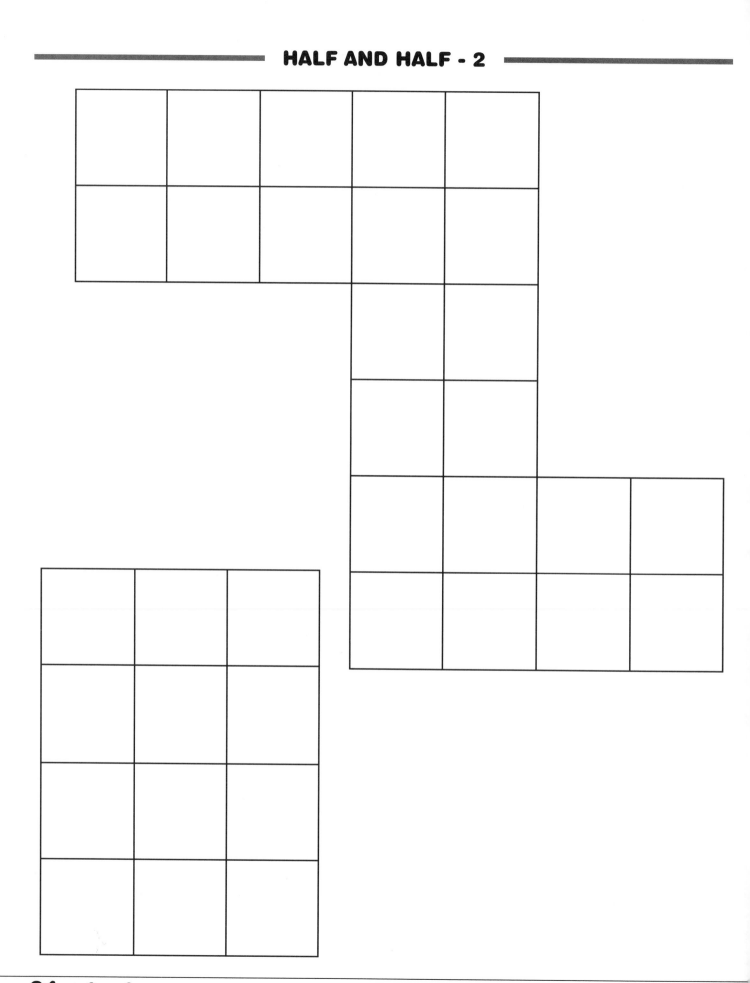

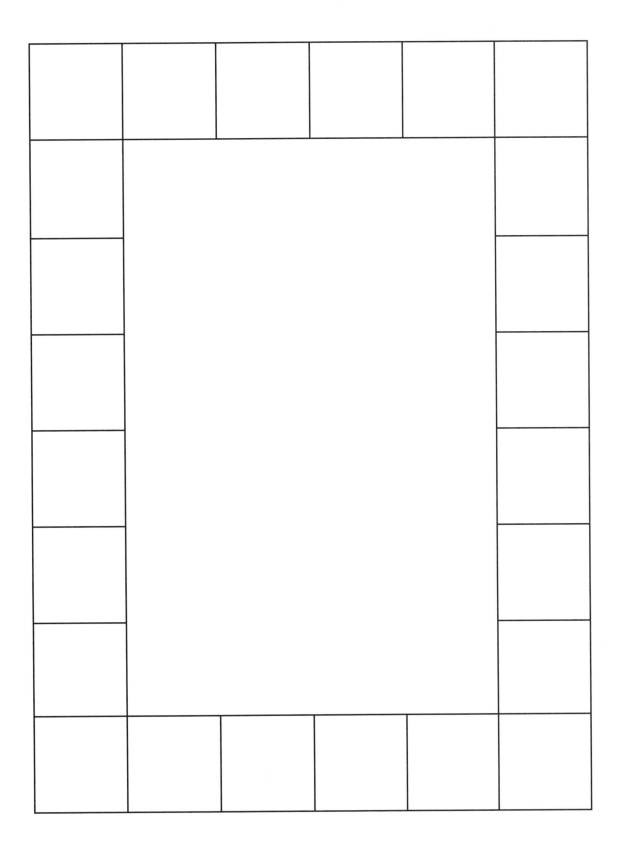

Mystery Pattern #1 Clues

1. It is an ABC pattern.

2. It doesn't have green.

3. Yellow comes first.

4. Red comes last.

Mystery Pattern #2 Clues

1. It is an AB pattern.

2. A is not red.

3. The second tile is green.

4. The name of the first color begins with a Y.

Mystery Pattern #3 Clues

1. It is an ABC pattern.

2. It has blue.

3. Yellow is A.

4. C is not red.

Mystery Pattern #4 Clues

1. It has 3 colors.

2. There is no red.

3. The name of the last color begins with a Y.

4. The middle color is not green.

Clue Cards #1, 2 are easy; #3, 4, 5 are harder; and #7, 8 are hardest.

Answer Key: Clue card #1 – yellow, blue, red
Clue card #2 – yellow, green

Clue card #3 – (three possible solutions)
yellow, red, blue; yellow, blue, green;
yellow, green, blue
Clue card # 4 – green, blue, yellow

Mystery Pattern #5 Clues

1. It is an ABCD pattern.

2. C is yellow.

3. The name of the first color begins with a B.

4. The second color is not red.

Mystery Pattern #6 Clues

1. It is an ABCD pattern.

2. B is red.

3. The third color is not green.

4. The last tile is yellow.

Mystery Pattern #7 Clues

1. It has 3 colors.

2. Every other tile is red.

3. Green is second.

4. There is no yellow.

Mystery Pattern #8 Clues

1. It has 2 colors.

2. The second and third tiles are the same color.

3. The first tile is not yellow.

4. B is green.

Clue Cards #1, 2 are easy; #3, 4, 5 are harder; and #7, 8 are hardest.

Clue card #7 — red, green, red, blue
Clue card # 8 — (two solutions)

Answer Key: Clue card #5 – blue, green, yellow, red
Clue card #6 – green, red, blue, yellow

blue, green, green
red, green, green

Brownie

Rusty

Sparky

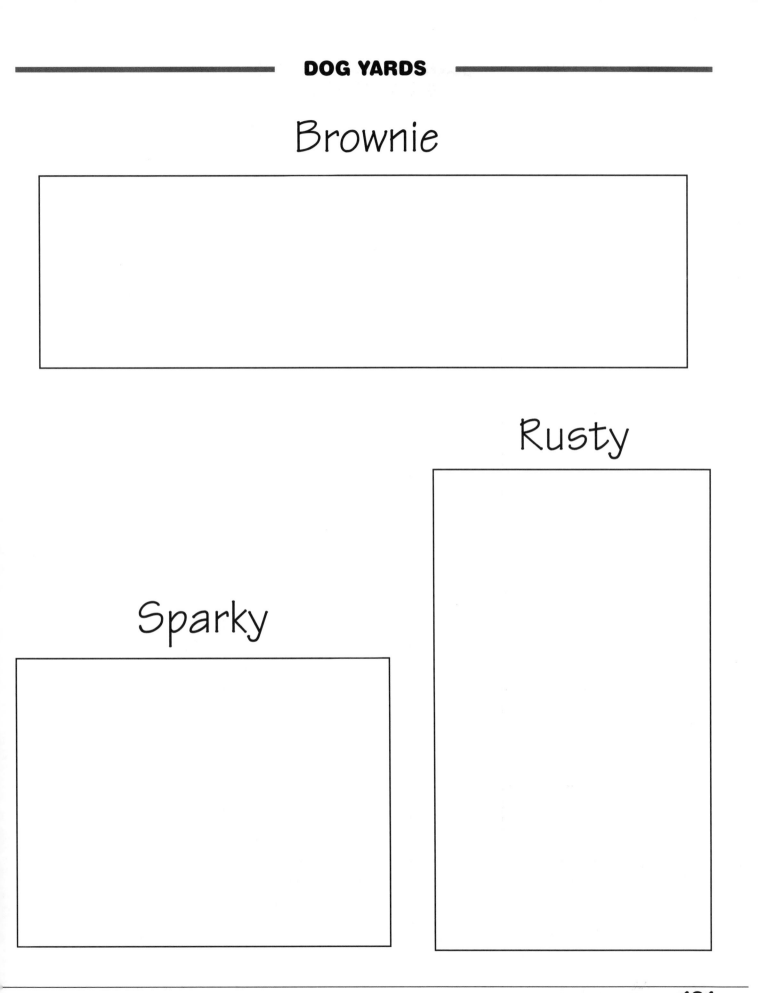

COLOR TILE GRID PAPER

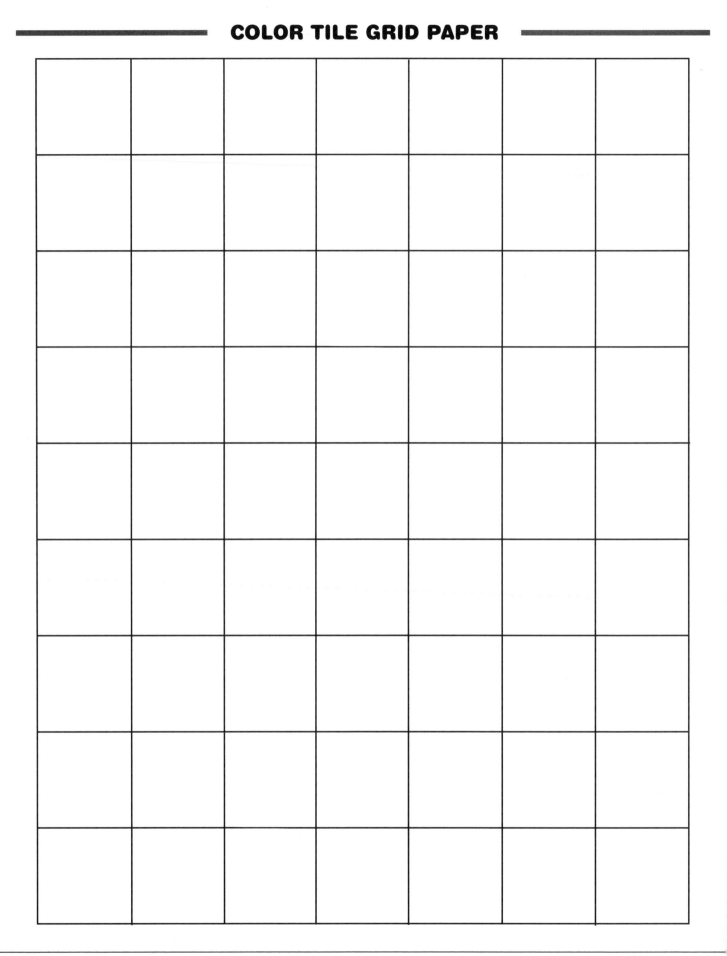

COLOR TILE WRITING PAPER

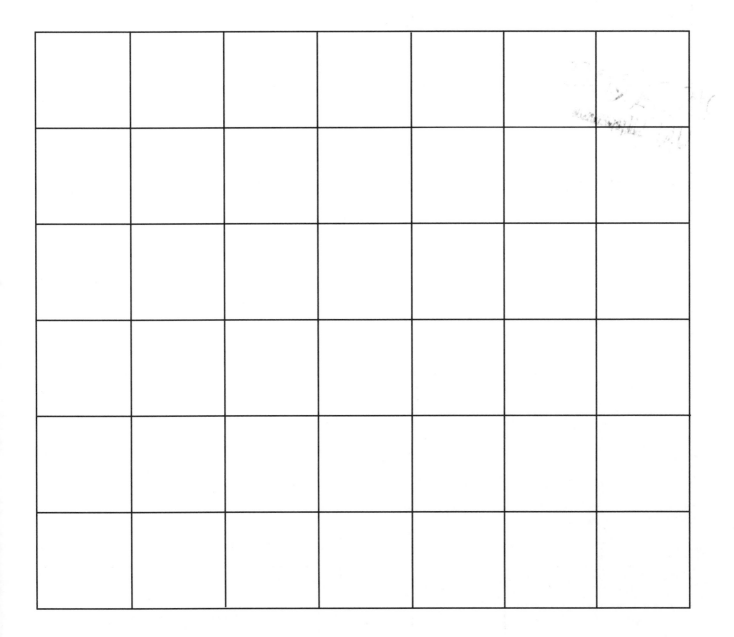